INTRODUCING

CHRISTIANITY

D0774585

Other Titles in This Series

INTRODUCING

CHRISTIANITY

Sally Bruyneel
and
Alan G. Padgett

ORBIS BOOKS

Maryknoll, New York 10545

Founded in 1970, Orbis Books endeavors to publish works that enlighten the mind, nourish the spirit, and challenge the conscience. The publishing arm of the Maryknoll Fathers and Brothers, Orbis seeks to explore the global dimensions of the Christian faith and mission, to invite dialogue with diverse cultures and religious traditions, and to serve the cause of reconciliation and peace. The books published reflect the opinions of their authors and are not meant to represent the official position of the Maryknoll Society. To obtain more information about Maryknoll and Orbis Books, please visit our website at www.maryknoll.org.

Library of Congress Cataloging-in-Publication Data
Bruyneel, Sally.
    Introducing Christianity / Sally Bruyneel and Alan G. Padgett.
        p.   cm.
    Includes bibliographical references and index.
    ISBN 1-57075-395-4 (pbk.)
    1. Christianity.   I. Padgett, Alan G.   II. Title.
BR121.3 .B78 2003
230 – dc21

                                                        2002155439

To Luke,
from whom we have learned so much

Contents

Preface

This book arose out of our experience as teachers of undergraduates in a small university. We realized that an older assumption, that even non-Christians know something about Christianity simply by virtue of being immersed in American culture, no longer was valid. We sensed the need for a basic book on Christianity that made no assumptions about the reader's knowledge of religion. It quickly became apparent that the primary hurdle for us in undertaking such a task is to respect the immensity of the subject and the intensity of people's feelings about it, while still remaining true to the vision of a simple introduction. Bill Burrows, of Orbis Books, understood this more clearly than most, and we are grateful for his encouragement and insight. Without him, this book would not have come to be.

We thank our students at Azusa Pacific University for their input in reading over an early draft of this work, especially our friends and former students Ashanti Austin and Lisa Welch. Jeanne Dahl, at Luther Seminary, also read over the manuscript and helped with the glossary. Thank you, Jeanne. Thanks also go to the people of Luther Seminary, who have supported our work and encouraged our writing. Any benefit the reader may derive from this work is largely a product of their good efforts. Omissions and errors may be left on our doorstep.

We dedicate this book to our son Luke, a gift from God and a great source of joy in our lives. *Deo Gratias.*

SB & AGP
Epiphany, 2003

Chapter 1

Introduction

Christianity is one of the great religions of the world. With millions of adherents worldwide, it is the faith of humble laborers and powerful leaders of nations. This faith has shaped the course of human history and affected the destinies of people on all seven continents. The Christian holy book, the Bible, is the most extensively translated text of all time, and Western civilization cannot be understood without it. Because of this, it is essential for the educated citizen of today's global village to develop a familiarity with the history and beliefs of the Christian faith. So how do we go about studying a religion whose followers speak a myriad of languages, populate countless cultures, and belong to every social class? What things do we need to know in order to understand Christianity? Does a religion with so many different ways of worshiping actually have a common set of beliefs? If so, what do Christians believe, and why? Where do we begin?

In this brief book we set out the things essential for an understanding of Christianity. This study is approached from the perspective of an inquirer, a person who is exploring the history, beliefs, and practices of the Christian religion. The purpose of this book is to introduce Christianity to readers who may be unfamiliar with the larger background, history, and doctrines of this important and ancient faith. Whether you are a Christian looking to become more grounded in your faith, or a student seeking to understand the religion that preeminently has shaped

1

the Western world, this book will give you a solid start. Whatever your motivation for reading this book, you can improve
your grasp of essential Christian teachings by working through
the material presented here.

In the chapters that follow we will learn about Christians and
the faith they embrace. We will cover the Christian practices,
beliefs, and traditions that are central to this distinctive world
religion. We also will look at the history of this faith and the
holy book that guides it. Finally, we will try to provide some
idea of what it means to live the Christian life. Of course, this
book cannot take the place of speaking with exemplary practi-
tioners of the Christian faith, which you may find represented
in your own community. But when you are through reading this
text, you will have a better grasp of what the Christian way of
life is all about.

We have written *Introducing Christianity* for inquirers interested in a concise introduction to the Christian tradition. This
text is aimed at entry-level college students and adult learners,
and assumes only a background familiarity with Western culture in general. Our goal is to provide a readable and reliable
interpretation of the most widely held of the world's religious
traditions. In creating this treatment of the Christian faith, we
recognize that no exercise of this nature can be free of biases.
The reader brings his or her own background and priorities to
the text, as do the authors. We, the authors of this text, are
unapologetically Christian, but we are also teachers who have
made every effort to step outside of our identity as Christians
and Americans in order to ask the questions that best serve the
quest for better understanding. It is our hope that the book you
now hold presents a balanced picture — one that does not flinch
from speaking of Christian shortcomings, but one that also
presents Christian ideals, even those that believers sometimes
fail to live up to.

Our goal is neither to create converts to a particular set of religious beliefs nor to bring readers into affiliation with any particular denominational expression of the Christian faith. Nevertheless, you will find that we as the authors take Christianity seriously. It is the religious belief system that guides our lives and informs our understanding of the world. We believe that this "insider" view of Christianity puts us in an excellent position to speak carefully and insightfully about the history, beliefs, and practices that are central to the followers of Jesus Christ. A simplistic approach that presents Christianity as just one more consumer option in a smorgasbord of personal preferences would not adequately capture the central tenet of this faith. Instead, we present Christianity as we know it: a living tradition, energized inwardly through faith and outwardly through diversity. This tradition centers upon total dedication to God, lived out in the context of the human community.

As we explore what it means to be part of the Christian faith, a number of concepts and terms appear that you may be encountering for the first time. To aid readers in gaining a rapid mastery of basic ideas, every chapter includes definitions and examples. These definitions are also included in a glossary of key terms, located after the last chapter. In addition, discussion questions for reflection and dialogue appear at the end of each section. Finally, suggestions for further reading are provided at the end of the book. We hope that reading this text stimulates your appetite for more in-depth reading about the Christian faith. In this way, we hope that the book may serve as a guide to further study on your own.

A word about the World Wide Web or Internet: We have found the shape of this powerful tool to be so shifting and changing that we fear that any Web sites listed in print will soon be out of date. We recommend seeking religious information on the Web from established sites run by universities, colleges, libraries, and church organizations. There is more junk than jewelry on the Net, and for some reason religion is a topic that particularly brings out the bizarre in cyberspace. So read with a critical eye, just as you should any source. Nevertheless, a lot of valuable information about Christianity is available on the Web.

To Begin With: Some Basic Concepts

The terms, questions, and bibliographic information provided in this text have been carefully chosen in order to introduce the concepts that are basic to understanding Christianity. Of course, the first word you should know is *religion.** A religion is a distinctive way of life that involves special practices and rituals, along with associated beliefs about the world and God or Ultimate Reality. Not all religions believe in gods, but all have some kind of worldview, or philosophy of life. A religion also entails an experience of a dimension that writers on religion have called "holy" and "sacred." Religion involves a relationship to that which is sacred and holy, even though the shape of the sacred is diverse in the many different kinds of religious life. For the people who believe it and live it, this philosophy of life helps make sense of the world. We say "believe it and live it" because a religion is not just a set of abstract ideas; it is a way of living life, and of seeing everything from a certain perspective.

What, then, are we talking about when we use the term "the Christian religion"? The Christian religion is a way of life centered on the life and teachings of a man, Jesus of Nazareth. He was born about two thousand years ago in Israel, into a family of humble laborers. Jesus' followers believe that he was sent from heaven to show humankind what God is like, and how

---

*Throughout the book, when we introduce concepts that may be unfamiliar, we will set them off in *bold italics.* See the glossary for definitions of and more information on these terms.

God wants people to live. For this reason, Jesus' first followers often called him *Messiah,* a Hebrew word meaning "anointed one" of God. In Greek, this word is *Christ,* and it is here that we get the word *Christian.* Christians are followers of Jesus the Messiah.

As we will see, Christians consider themselves to be one great family, or body of believers, called the *church.* This family cannot be defined by geography, race, language, or any of the other ways by which we usually identify a human community. Instead, Christians believe that they have been united through the power of God's Spirit. They believe that following the teachings of Jesus is the best way to serve God. This *faith* teaches that all of life should be lived as an expression of love and obedience to God. Christians are taught in their holy book that they should worship God in all they do. To worship is to show honor or reverence for God. Christians understand themselves, therefore, to be worshipers of God. This focus on worship is central to the faith, and is an organizing principle for the Christian life. In the attempt to honor God in all aspects of human life, all of life can become a kind of worship. However, Christians also gather for a special time of worship, most often on Sunday mornings. When they come together for worship, they frequently meet in a special building dedicated to honoring God. This place is commonly referred to as a "church" because it is the place where Christ's family, the church, meets. In such meetings, believers worship God in explicit ways through praying, singing, teaching, preaching, and fellowship.

From the time of the first Christians until now, worship has included a number of religious rituals. A *ritual* is a traditional practice or ceremony that has symbolic or spiritual meaning. Although rituals differ somewhat among various groups of Christians, they do practice many things in common. All Christians pray and read the *Bible,* their holy book, also referred to as "Scripture" (the "writings"). Christians sing religious songs, called *hymns,* in their meetings. Often, worship includes a *sermon,* a talk that explains and applies the meaning of the Bible. The person giving this talk is preaching, explaining the good news of Jesus Christ and how it applies to our lives today. Most often, the people who give these talks during worship are the leaders of the local Christian group. These men and women are the pastors, priests, or preachers who guide the local Christian fellowship. In addition to the practices mentioned already, there are also special rituals known as *sacraments.* Unlike those Christian practices that invite all to participate, sacraments are reserved for those who are followers of Jesus Christ. These special rituals include *baptism* and *Holy Communion.*

Worship, preaching, and sacraments are practices that have their foundations in the teachings of the Bible. As we have already mentioned, the Bible (from a Latin word meaning "books") is the Christian holy book. It contains two parts: the Old Testament and the New Testament. The man Jesus was a Jew, and the Old Testament contains the holy books of the Jews, the *Hebrew* Bible. This first part tells the story of God and God's people, Israel. It contains many laws, stories, poems, and wise sayings, and is the larger part of the Bible. The second part is the New Testament, based upon the life and teachings of Jesus. It contains four *Gospels,* which tell us about Jesus, his life, ministry, and death. It also contains a number of epistles, letters written by his most trusted disciples to members of the early church. The Bible is extremely important to the Christian faith because it includes rules and principles given to human beings by God, especially in the teachings of Jesus Christ. However, for Christians, the Bible is more than just a book of rules; it is the faithful record of God's relationship with human beings throughout many generations, and it gives Christians a common source of teaching. With almost two billion Christians on earth today, the Bible is one thing that all Christians have in common.

Just as there are many different languages and cultures on earth, so also there are many types of Christian churches all over the world. But Christianity started long ago, among a small group of Jews in Palestine. The early church, however, grew rapidly, and within four hundred years it had spread throughout the known world. This development was already diverse, encompassing the lands we now call Africa, the Middle East, Asia, and Europe. Over time, three broad types of Christianity evolved. The Eastern *Orthodox* and the Roman *Catholic* churches are the oldest, with roots going back to the earliest Christian groups. The third type, the *Protestant* church, is a loose collection of independent groups. Protestant churches have their roots in a kind of Christianity that broke away from the Roman Catholic Church in order to reform religious faith and practice. There are many types of Protestant worship today, practiced by groups with names such as *Lutheran, Baptist, Anglican, Presbyterian, Methodist,* and *Congregationalist.* These groups, or *denominations,* all trace their beginnings to Christ's ministry on earth, just as the Orthodox and the Catholics do. All consider themselves to be members of the "body of Christ," which is another way of referring to the church. This way of speaking reminds believers that they are to join together into one entity to do the work of Christ and to live as he taught. Every follower of Christ, whether Orthodox, Catholic, or Protestant, is bound by this commitment to the life and teachings of Christ.

The question of what is essential to the character of true Christianity and how it is to be practiced has often led the church into conflict. Sometimes the disagreement has been among Christians themselves. At other times it was with government rulers or with other religious groups. These various struggles and conflicts influenced the development of the church. For example, several official councils, or meetings of church leaders, helped to define Christian teaching and *doctrine.* Doctrines are principles or beliefs of the church, and include subjects such as God, Jesus, the Holy Spirit, and Christian worship. These early councils of the church focused primarily on *theology*. Theology is the study of God, whereby the church seeks to honor God through contemplating and understanding God's true nature. Because Christianity seeks to know the truth about God, the church takes theology very seriously. However, the life of faith is not just about knowing God; it is about faithfully serving God through appropriate actions.

Christianity holds that human beings should act in ways that conform to the ethical teachings of Jesus Christ. For believers, theology and life are not separate realms segregated from one another. Although Christianity presents a variety of options in theology and ethics, Christians agree that theology and life should go together. In the growth of the church, early leaders were focused on the faithful practice of the Christian life. Doctrinal standards were defined and developed largely as a response to teachings that violated the spirit of *traditions* carefully tended since Jesus' time on earth. This touches upon a delicate point among churches. We seek throughout this book to be honest to the history and reality of Christian religion, even if that means making observations that are difficult for some believers to accept. The most pressing and obvious observation is that churches sometimes disagree about how to interpret particular sections of Scripture, and this has been a source of division in the church. These conflicts sometimes have given rise to the formulation of specific doctrinal differences, many of which still remain in our own day and age. These differences in *dogma* — theological teachings of church authorities — have often produced groups of believers who feel that they can no longer remain in communion with those from whom they differ. On the other hand, many of the difficulties that have arisen in the church throughout the centuries are due less to disputes about Scripture than to unwillingness to obey its clearest teachings.

With these introductory remarks in mind, we can begin our examination of the Christian faith. Our first area of focus is

Christian worship, which we consider from the perspective of sacred time and sacred space. We begin here because such worship is a contemporary behavior that sets Christian believers apart. Building upon this, we then turn our attention to the one in whose name Christians worship — Jesus Christ. With this background, we are in a better position to understand the significance of the Christian sacred book, the Bible. From our discussion of the Bible, the text moves into an overview of *church history.* In our chapters on the history of the church we look first to the common roots of all Christian churches. From there we trace the growth of the faith, its spread across the globe, and its development into the diverse family of believers that represents the faith today. We finish our exploration with a survey of common Christian theology and ethical teachings.

Questions for Further Reflection

1. What do you find interesting about Christianity?
2. What is the difference between a religion and a denomination?
3. The Bible is an ancient book. How is it possible for the Bible to speak to modern women and men?
4. All world religions, including Christianity, have some kind of theology or religious doctrine. Why is this so?
5. If you were going to describe Christianity to someone, based on your experience with Christians, what would you say?
6. Would you say that you are religious? What special practices and rituals do you have that inform others as to your worldview or philosophy of life?

Chapter 2

Sacred Time, Sacred Space

Religions give people an orientation to life, a way of placing themselves and their world in perspective. Religious beliefs and practices reflect an awareness that human beings are connected with something larger than themselves. This religious experience, and the beliefs and rituals that arise from it, are described as "sacred." To call something sacred is to say that it is set apart for religious purposes. Most religions have special places, such as shrines or temples, that are set apart for practices associated with the spiritual life. Sacred spaces usually are devoted to worship and ritual, or to other events that have religious significance. The events themselves also can be sacred, in the sense that they are times set apart for religious purposes. In this chapter we will use these ideas of sacred time and sacred space to gain a better understanding of what Jesus' followers believe. Our starting point will be the Christian conception of time. We also will look at the seasons of the Christian calendar and explain their symbolic meaning. From there the discussion will turn to the places that are sacred for the faith of Christians and to the practices associated with their sacred space.

Sacred Time

All religions have a perception of time that is shaped by their understanding of human existence. In Genesis, the first

Because of the obvious religious meaning of
B.C. and A.D., secular historians sometimes
date events as C.E. and B.C.E., meaning
"Common Era" and "Before the Common
Era." The actual dates remain the same,
whether we write A.D. or C.E. For example,
Rome fell to the Goths in A.D. 410 or 410 C.E.

book of the Bible, we read, "In the beginning, God created the heaven and the earth." For this reason, Christians view time as something with a specific beginning or starting point. Likewise, the followers of Christ believe that time as we now experience it will also have an end. Revelation, the last book of the Bible, tells of a time when "the first heaven and the first earth" will cease to exist. Because Scripture presents human history as something that moves forward from a beginning to an end, the Christian conception of time is linear. In addition, the church has developed its own particular way of marking the passing of time. In the Christian faith, human history is organized according to its distance from the birth of Jesus Christ. For this reason, Christians label all of time before Jesus as *B.C.*, for "Before Christ." For example, 500 B.C. means five hundred years before the birth of Christ. Years that follow the birth of Jesus are labeled *A.D.*, for *Anno Domini*, which is Latin for "in the year of the Lord." Thus, A.D. 500 refers to a time five hundred years after Christ was born. For the Christian, then, all of history centers on Jesus Christ. Because this faith has been so influential in history, particularly in the West, this Christian way of dating historical events has become the common international method. It is important to realize, however, that many cultures and religions also use different dating systems.

In addition to the Christian calendar, which has become the international standard for dating and recording world events, the church also has its own seasons of the year. These seasons of the church calendar focus on Jesus Christ and his mission in this world. Christians use this as a way to honor the memory of Jesus' life on earth. This calendar sets apart different times of the year to focus upon Jesus' birth, his ministry on earth, his death and *resurrection,* and the promise that he will always be present with the church. In this way, Jesus' followers use sacred time as a way to focus upon him in order to keep him at the center of their daily lives. Some Christian seasons are familiar to almost everyone. For example, *Christmas,* a season that celebrates the birth of Christ, is well known to most people. Indeed, it has become so popular that people of other religions sometimes celebrate it. However, other sacred times are likely to receive less notice, even among Christians. For example, the season of *Epiphany,* a period in which the church celebrates God coming into the world, often receives little attention. Despite this, the seasons of the Christian calendar are intended to remind people about the events that are significant for the Christian faith. It is therefore a good source of information for anyone seeking an increased understanding of this important faith.

The Christian year begins with *Advent,* which usually starts in early December, just before Christmas. Advent is the season of waiting, during which texts from the earlier part of the Bible, the Old Testament, are read in church. Such Bible lessons focus on the anticipation of the Hebrew people (the Jews) for the coming of the Messiah. This season is one in which the anticipation of the coming of Christ into the world is often symbolized by candles. Many churches will make an "Advent wreath," with four candles representing the number of weeks until Christmas. A fifth, central candle of the wreath is larger than the others, and is white. It is called the "Christ candle" and will be lit only at Christmas. The color for church vestments and decorations during Advent is purple.

Christmas is the next season of the Christian year, and its color is white. The feast day itself is always December 25, but celebration of the birth of Christ lasts for two weeks, as is reflected in traditional songs in the West such as "The Twelve Days of Christmas." As that song suggests, it is a time for giving and receiving gifts. Gifts are given as a reminder that at Christmas, God gave the world the gift of Jesus Christ, the Savior. Although it is unfortunate that gifts have become the focus of this Western holiday, Christmas is still a time when the world focuses upon peace and kindness toward others.

The Christian Year		
Name	*Typical Month*	*Common Color*
Advent	December*	Purple
Christmas	December	White
Epiphany	January	White
Lent	March*	Purple
Good Friday	April*	Black or Red
Easter	April*	White
Pentecost	June*	Red

After the Christmas season, at the start of the new calendar year in January, the church observes the little-known season of Epiphany. This celebrates the belief that in the person of Jesus Christ, God has entered human history in a unique way. The word "epiphany" means a personal revelation of the divine (in this case, the Christian God). During Epiphany, the church also

*Exact dates for these festivals change from year to year.

remembers the coming of the magi ("wise men") to the baby Jesus. The story of the magi is found in the Gospel of Matthew, the first book of the New Testament. It represents the idea that in Jesus, God has come into history for the whole world. This is because the magi are thought to have come from far outside the Jewish nation. Thus, they have become a *symbol* for the entire world outside of Israel.

Lent is the next Christian season after Epiphany. This season takes up an important event in the life of Jesus when he journeyed alone into the wilderness. According to the Gospels, there he was tempted by Satan to abandon his mission. The word "Lent" comes from an Old English word meaning "spring," for Lent takes place in the springtime. After Christmas and *Easter,* Lent is probably the most well-known season of the Christian year. Lent is the season in which Christians prepare to celebrate Easter. It calls to mind the time of fasting and self-denial that Jesus went through at the start of his journey to his death and resurrection. During Lent it is traditional for Christians in many churches to fast and pray as a way to join spiritually with Jesus in his suffering and fasting in the wilderness. Because it is a time of self-denial that many dreaded, it also became a custom to celebrate the Tuesday before Lent begins as Mardi Gras — literally, "fat Tuesday" (also known as "pancake Tuesday" in some places) — now a popular secular festival in many countries.

Ash Wednesday, the first day of Lent, is always forty days before Easter. Lent is a time when Christians are supposed to deny the world and worldly pleasures in order to focus on spiritual growth and on their relationship with God and their neighbors.

At the end of Lent is *Holy Week,* a weeklong period of solemn remembrance that ends with the celebration of Easter — one of the high points of the Christian year. Holy Week starts on *Palm Sunday,* the Sunday before Easter. This day recalls Jesus' entrance into Jerusalem during which the people praised him and threw palm leaves down before him to honor his coming. That is why the branches of palm trees are often given to those worshiping in church on this special day. Another special day in Holy Week is **Good Friday** (sometimes called "Black Friday"), when the church remembers the death of Jesus on the cross. This is a special day of fasting and *prayer* for Christians, and its color is black. Although this is a quiet day given to reflection upon the suffering that Christ endured for humankind, it is also a time of hope and joy for believers.

Christ's followers experience a feeling of anticipation and gladness as they prepare to celebrate Easter. Easter is the most joyous and important season of the Christian calendar. During Easter the church celebrates Jesus' resurrection. The word "resurrection" simply means "to rise again," and here it refers to the belief that Jesus Christ rose from the dead three days after he was buried. This is celebrated on Easter Sunday, at the end of Holy Week. Like Christmas, Easter is a joyous time that is celebrated by many people, even by many who do not profess the Christian faith. In the West, this time is associated with spring. Not surprisingly, the holiday has become a time for gathering together to celebrate the newness of life that fills the earth as winter passes. Churches are often specially decorated for Easter. Black or purple decorations give way to white and gold. Flowers decorate the church inside and out. The change from the quiet sadness of Holy Week to the enthusiasm and joy of Easter is quite dramatic, and the church is filled with excitement and praise for God.

Special services are also held to celebrate the fulfillment of God's promise in the resurrection of Christ. In some traditions, believers gather at midnight in the dark, each person holding an unlit candle. In the darkness outside the church door a fire is kindled and a candle lit. A leader enters the church with a single candle casting its light across the darkness. This symbolizes the light of Christ conquering the darkness and death. The single flame is passed around, and from that single flame all

the candles held by the other worshipers are lit. In other traditions, sunrise services are held early on Easter morning, when
believers gather in the gray morning just before the sun rises.
There they worship God and anticipate the rising of the sun as a
symbol of Christ's own resurrection from the grave. Like the lit
candle, this is symbolic of Christ defeating death and bringing
light to the world.

After the Easter season comes **Pentecost.** Always fifty days
after Easter, Pentecost is observed as a time when Jesus Christ
sent the Holy Spirit to his followers. For Christians, the Holy
Spirit is God, living today in the life and worship of the faithful
and at work in the world. The coming of the Holy Spirit on the
first Pentecost long ago is often referred to as the "birthday of the
church." Described in the New Testament book the Acts of the
Apostles, Pentecost speaks of a time when the Spirit of God came
upon Christ's followers in a new and powerful way. Pentecost is
the last season of the Christian year, and it is the longest.

The season after Pentecost extends until the beginning of Advent and is sometimes known as "ordinary time." A key feast in
this period of ordinary time occurs on the second Sunday after
Pentecost: Trinity Sunday. This feast introduces the Christian
belief that God, while being one, in acting to create, save, and
live within people, is revealed to be three: Father, Son, and Holy
Spirit. This is the concept of the *Trinity,* which we will discuss
later in the book. The season of ordinary time brings us to the
end of the Christian year.

Just as the Christian year focuses upon the life and work of
Jesus Christ, so does the week. On Sunday, the first day of the
week, the church comes together to honor God. Because Christians believe that this was the day on which Jesus rose from
the dead, they have gathered to worship God on Sunday for almost two thousand years. Although worship of Jesus Christ can
take place anywhere, this weekly gathering usually takes place
in a special building dedicated to the worship of God. This is

a sacred space for Christians, a place set apart for God and God's people. In the section that follows we will discuss the special places where Christians meet. Our discussion will include a description of the buildings and an explanation of the special furnishings inside them.

Sacred Space

As we have already mentioned, the church is a way of referring to those who believe in the Christian faith. It is a group of people around the world, joined together by their belief that Jesus Christ is a unique revelation of God's truth; the church is the people who gather to worship him. However, over time the term "church" also has come to mean a building in which Christians worship. This can be confusing for those new to the study of Christianity, but the distinction quickly becomes familiar. The places where Christians worship are as diverse as the people who use them. There is no rule about what kind of structure can become a church. The size and shape of churches range from very small buildings known as chapels, to huge cathedrals located in large cities. In fact, some Christians meet in what is called a "house church," a local worshiping community that convenes in someone's home. As we will see in many other aspects in this introduction to Christianity, the followers of Jesus have many different ideas about how best to put his teaching and example into practice. However, for most of the Christian groups throughout the world today, a special building is set apart for worshiping God.

Church buildings can be very large indeed, or rather small. Despite the great variety, some similarities exist. There are places for people to sit or to stand, and a special place where most of the religious rituals will take place. This central place for worship is called a *sanctuary,* which comes from a Latin word meaning "sacred place." The sanctuary usually has an altar (or table) and a pulpit (or podium). Most churches also have a variety of Christian symbols and art both outside and inside the building. The most universal symbol is a cross, a reminder of Jesus' death and resurrection. In some traditions, the cross has a representation of Jesus attached to it. It is then called a "crucifix." Usually candles, or other types of light, are used to symbolize God's presence. The church may also include art such as sculpture, statues, stained glass, or paintings that remind Christians of important events or teachings. Here we find stories of God's faithfulness to his people, of Jesus Christ and his ministry, of Mary his mother, or of the apostles and other great leaders of the church. In some traditions stylized portraits called *icons* are included in places of worship.

Icons, statues, and other works of art serve to remind Christians of those who have gone before them in the faith. They are reminders of God's faithfulness, past and present. Every Christian is part of a much larger community, which has an important history. These leaders and heroes of the church's past are sometimes called "saints." All of these things may be used in sacred space as a way to help people focus upon the wonderful work of God, and humanity's place in it.

The Church Building: Some Key Vocabulary

Some parts of a church building have special, old names that are still used. The narthex or foyer is the entrance hall or lobby that you come into as you enter a church building. The nave is the central part of the church, where most of the people sit or stand. In the main body of the church are some common points of reference for the believer. In the main sanctuary area we usually find the altar, a special table used in Christian rituals. For example, this is where the bread and wine for Holy Communion are placed before being blessed and distributed. Near the altar is the pulpit, usually a large podium or stand. From here leaders pray, preach a sermon, or address the worshipers on behalf of the church. The sermon (or homily) is a spoken message that helps people apply the meaning of the Bible to their lives. To the left of the pulpit there is usually a lectern, a smaller podium or stand. This is the place where Scripture is read to the congregation. In some churches, however, the same stand serves as both pulpit and lectern.

The *congregation,* a group of people assembled to worship God, may sit, stand, or kneel facing the altar or the pulpit. Usually the congregants (those who come to worship) sit together in pews (rows of benches) or chairs in the nave or main body of the church building. The nave leads up to a chancel, where the altar and the pulpit are located. The chancel is the front part of a church building and is often where the choir sings during the service. Finally, many church buildings have a tall steeple or spire that tapers upward to a point with a cross at the top. These older, traditional vocabulary terms sometimes are forgotten in modern churches, but they are used quite commonly in reference to older church buildings. Whatever the church looks like, it remains a place where people gather to honor God. The whole of a church building is devoted to the worship of God.

Christian Symbols You Should Know

The Christian religion began during the time of the Roman Empire. Then, as now, believers came from many different social, cultural, and ethnic backgrounds. Though Greek and Latin provided common languages for communication, government, and commerce across the empire, many people were unable to read or write either of them. Symbols such as the fish and the cross became a way of representing important Christian ideas and teachings, even for believers who had no education. These symbols also were used to identify Christians to one another, especially during times when believers were persecuted by the empire. Today the cross, long identified with Christ and his followers, is one of the most widely recognized symbols in the world.

 The cross is a fundamental symbol of Christ. It was the instrument used to kill him on Good Friday, and has become the most common Christian symbol.

 These are the first and last letters in the Greek alphabet, *alpha* and *omega*. Jesus said, "I am the Alpha and the Omega, the first and the last, the beginning and the end" (Revelation 22:13). These letters stand for his eternal life.

 The dove is a symbol of the Holy Spirit. This is because a dove landed on Jesus at his baptism, symbolizing the fullness of the Holy Spirit in his life (Mark 1:10).

Another symbol of the Holy Spirit is a flame. Flames of fire appeared above the followers of Jesus when the Holy Spirit came to them at Pentecost (Acts 2:3; cf. Luke 3:16).

 A ship, especially with a mast that forms a cross, is often used as a symbol of the church.

 An open book is a symbol for the Bible. Two tables of stone symbolize the Ten Commandments, a well-known part of the Bible.

The lamb is a symbol both of the followers of Jesus, "the Good Shepherd" (John 10:11), and of Jesus himself, "the Lamb of God who takes away the sin of the world" (John 1:29). When the lamb is used as a symbol of Jesus, it usually is shown with a cross of some kind.

 Along with the cross, the fish is one of the oldest symbols of Christ. In the Greek language, spoken by the early church, the first letters of the five words "Jesus Christ, God's Son, Savior" spell the word "fish" (*ichthys*).

 A figure having a shape with three parts, such as a triangle or a shamrock with three leaves, is used as a symbol for God the Trinity — one God being Father, Son, and Holy Spirit.

All of these symbols are part of the history and tradition of Christianity. They have special significance for the followers of Christ because they are reminders of God's truth. They also remind believers of their heritage in a family of faith that stretches back through time and bears witness to God's enduring faithfulness. Because of the rich resources that symbols provide, they often adorn the places where Christians gather.

Questions for Further Reflection

1. Which symbol do you most associate with the Christian faith, and why?

2. If you were asked to create a symbol to represent Christianity, what would it look like, and why?

3. Have you ever entered a place or "space" that felt sacred? Describe that experience. What are some of the things that made that place special?

4. Have you ever been in a church building? In what ways did it resemble, and in what ways did it differ from, a traditional church?

Chapter 3

Christian Worship

Religious practice is central to the Christian faith and emphasizes the concept of devotion to God in every aspect of human life. Christians believe in a personal God, who created everything that exists. According to the Bible, God is a holy being characterized by love, justice, and mercy. God calls all people into a relationship with him and enables them to live in accordance with the divine will. As we saw in the preceding chapter, one way in which Christians explore and enjoy the presence of God is through worship. They believe that in worship, human beings actually encounter the divine creator and sustainer of human life. This practice of consciously seeking God is a sacred obligation and privilege for every member of the church. As you might imagine, this experience is different for each person, since each Christian has a personal and intimate relationship with God. Interestingly, this individual relationship with God brings with it the obligation to be in community with other Christians. Although Christians are called to spend time alone with God, they also are called to participate in the life of the church.

Christianity is most fully realized when believers are part of communities that help them grasp and obey God's will for their lives. One sign of this is the way in which followers of Christ are called to worship God together. The conscious expression of respect, love, and praise for God is supposed to fill both the public and the private lives of Christians. In this chapter, we will look at Christian worship as an open and visible group

23

practice, and as a personal and individual act of devotion. We will consider the practices of prayer, hymn singing, *liturgy,* and sacred rites or sacraments. Next, we will look at the concept of the church, using the models of community and family. We conclude with a brief description of different kinds of churches. Our discussion begins with corporate worship as an expression of the community of faith.

Corporate Worship

Although the faith teaches that each individual is responsible for honoring and obeying God, Christianity is most fully realized in community. Christians have gathered together to worship God since the first believers walked in Israel. Throughout the centuries this worship has reflected the unchanging nature of God and the diverse cultural settings in which Christian communities exist. When believers assemble for corporate worship, they meet together as a group in the name of Christ. Corporate worship is the collective expression of love and adoration for God. This corporate gathering of Christians is known as a congregation. Every local congregation of believers is considered to be part of one Christian body, the church. Although they meet together out of respect for God and obedience to Scripture, Christians also congregate for worship because of the special way they experience God when together. Through prayers, hymns, liturgy, and ritual they express their common devotion in a collective voice.

Christian worship always includes prayer, which is the act of talking to and listening for God. There are many different types of prayer. For example, people pray to give thanks, or to ask God for help or forgiveness. When Christians gather together, their prayers invite God to be present with them in a special way during worship. Prayer is also an acknowledgment

The Lord's Prayer

Our Father, who art in heaven,
hallowed be Thy name.
Thy kingdom come, Thy will be done
on earth as it is in heaven.
Give us this day our daily bread,
and forgive us our trespasses,
as we forgive those
who trespass against us.
And lead us not into temptation,
but deliver us from evil.

According to the New Testament, Jesus was asked to teach his followers how to pray. The prayer he taught them became known as the Lord's Prayer. Also known as the "Our Father" or "Pater Noster," it is often recited at public gatherings of the church.

of dependence upon God for all things. In prayer, believers open themselves to God. They make a *confession* of the wrong they have done, offer thanks for what God has given, and seek God's guidance in their lives. Worship also includes songs known as hymns. Hymns remind the faithful of God's love and power, and focus attention on God. These songs can be simple choruses of praise for God, or they can be sophisticated theological statements put to music. The word "liturgy," which comes from a Greek word meaning "work of the people," refers to formally structured worship in which the congregation participates in unison. The use of liturgy is another way in which believers can worship, addressing the needs and desires of the community in a common voice. This can include reading prayers and

psalms, recitations of a *creed,* or other worship that has a pre-
scribed form. In addition to prayers, hymns, and liturgy there
are rituals or religious acts that almost every church includes in
its worship service. Four of the most common rituals are Bible
reading, preaching, baptism, and Holy Communion.

Because the Bible is central to the Christian faith, it is read
in almost every worship service. After the Scripture reading,
someone discusses the Bible passage and explains what it means
for people today. This activity, called preaching, provides the
congregation with an opportunity to learn together. The talk
that the preacher (local pastor or priest) gives, the sermon or
homily, is based on a church teaching or a passage of Scripture. The sermon usually is presented by a leader of the local
church. This person is known as a pastor, priest (often addressed as "Father"), or minister. Different churches call their
leaders by different names, but these are usually easy to pick up
from others in the church service. The pastor also leads other
special rituals, or sacraments. The term "sacrament" comes
from a Latin word meaning "sacred oath," and it designates a
Christian practice performed with great seriousness and respect.
The two most universally practiced sacraments are baptism and
Holy Communion, which some churches call the *Eucharist.*

The Sacraments

In the sacrament of baptism, the individual believer openly
pledges to follow Christ and joins the church. At the same
time, the church makes a stated or implicit pledge to support
the believer in his or her walk of faith. This recognizes that
Christians have a responsibility to care for one another, just as
Christ cared for the church. In baptism, as with any sacrament,
there are two elements: physical and spiritual. In baptism, the

Christian Sacraments

Sacraments, or ordinances, as they are sometimes called, are practices based upon the Scripture and tradition of the Christian faith. The most widely recognized sacraments are:

- Baptism: A practice that represents a public declaration of faith. Here, the believer is partially or fully covered with water as a sign of new life in Christ and the regeneration of faith.

- Confirmation: A practice whereby a Christian, baptized as an infant, publicly acknowledges acceptance of the baptism.

- Eucharist: Also known as Holy Communion or the Lord's Supper. This ritual is a holy meal of bread and wine, symbolizing the body and blood of Christ.

- Penance: Also known as confession. This is the personal acknowledgment of sin, either in private or public.

- Sacrament of the Sick (at one time called "Extreme Unction"): The practice of anointing the seriously ill with oil, accompanied by prayers for healing.

- Holy Orders: Ordination to the office of deacon, priest, or bishop.

- Holy Matrimony: Marriage.

- Foot Washing: A practice of washing the feet of fellow Christians, symbolizing humility and the servanthood of Christ.

physical element is water, used to symbolize the spiritual purity, cleansing, and new life that come to the believer through Jesus Christ. This ritual, which has been practiced since the days when Jesus himself walked the earth, often takes place in a large body of water, such as a river or lake. Other churches may have a baptistery, a small indoor pool of water set apart for baptism. There, the candidate for baptism is immersed in the water and baptized in the name of God the Father, Son, and Holy Spirit. Another common practice is to baptize the new believer at a baptismal font, using just a few drops of water, usually applied to the forehead, again in the name of the Father, Son, and Holy Spirit. Some congregations baptize infants and young children, in which the faith of parents and/or sponsors is responding on behalf of the child, while others baptize only older children and adults, who are able to make their own professions of faith. In many churches that baptize infants, those children are expected later, when mature enough, to make a *confirmation* of their baptism. In every case, the local church performing the baptism is making a commitment to help the believer grow and develop in his or her life as a Christian.

The second major sacrament is Holy Communion, also called the Lord's Supper or the Eucharist. The physical part of this sacrament is bread and wine (or in many churches, unfermented grape juice), which is ingested in accordance with Christ's instruction. As is the case in many other Christian practices, different churches have different ways of celebrating Holy Communion. We describe the different kinds of churches more fully later in the chapter; for now, let us look at the three broad groups of Orthodox, Catholic, and Protestant. For Catholics and Orthodox, the Eucharist is celebrated in the midst of a more elaborate liturgy with singing and incense. In all cases in these churches, there is a union between two halves of the service. The first is called the "liturgy of the Word," with a focus on Scripture, and the second is called the "liturgy of the Eucharist." Among Protestants, the practice of Holy Communion runs the gamut from churches whose liturgies are as full of ceremony as those of the Orthodox and Catholic to churches whose liturgies are very simple. In all cases, though, the important thing is for the believer to dispose himself or herself to enter fully into communion with Jesus, who asked his followers to celebrate the event in his memory.

Like baptism, the sacrament of Holy Communion originates from the time of Jesus' life on earth. This act of eating and drinking is in memory of the last supper that Jesus had with his disciples, an event that he commanded them to continue in his name. When Christians eat the bread and drink from the cup, they are celebrating the communion between the individual, the church, and Christ. This act of communion also symbolizes the self-giving sacrifice of Jesus on the cross, when he gave himself up as an offering to God for the sins of humanity. Many Christians believe that the bread and wine actually become in some way the body and blood of Christ (although there is no visible change in them), while others believe that the bread and wine are symbols of the body and blood of Christ at the cross. Although only Christians may participate in Holy Communion and baptism, observers are welcome to be present during the sacrament.

Finally, although it is not a sacrament, an offering will be taken in almost all churches. This may come either early in the service or near the end. Whenever it takes place, the offering is a time when Christ's followers give money to help support the church and the work of God in the world. This collection is not a charge or fee for worship services, since Christ's life and death were given freely for all human beings. Christians give money and other gifts in church as a sign of obedience to God in all aspects of their lives and to show their commitment to the work of Christ in the world. It many ways it is symbolic of giving their lives — all they are and all they have — back to God, the creator. During the collection there may be an offertory hymn or procession. This usually is some type of vocal or instrumental music intended to help congregants experience giving as a type of worship. If you are in a church service during an offering, you may contribute as a sign of respect. However, visitors are not expected to give an offering, and the church does not force anyone to give.

Worship services commonly last about an hour, but many can last two hours or even longer. The formal worship ends with a *benediction,* or blessing, given to the congregation by the minister. The wording of a typical benediction asks God to bless the people as they return to their daily lives and to strengthen them to follow Christ in everything they say and do until they return again to worship. This prayer often invokes God as Father, Son, and Holy Spirit, the threefold name of God (we will learn more about the Trinity in a later chapter).

Many churches also include a time of fellowship after the worship service. Here, Christians can meet, talk, and continue building friendships with other believers. This is because a congregation is more than just a group of individuals who come together by choice. It is a chance for Christians to experience the unity that all believers are called to share as followers of Christ. Every person who professes Christ becomes united with the entire Christian family across the globe. A particular church is thus a local gathering place for an immense community of believers.

Beyond Sunday Morning

Christians believe that God created humankind to live, work, and play in ways that honor him. Because of this, churches often gather together at times other than Sunday morning.

Christians gather to study Scripture and Christian teaching in small groups or classes, they participate in projects to improve the community where they live, and they travel to work with orphans, the poor, and victims of natural disasters. This is how they express their love for God and their care for the world God created. And because the church includes people of all ages, Christians often have opportunities to gather together with others in their age group. This gives them a chance to worship, grow, and learn in ways that fit different stages of life. Christ's followers are called to nurture and encourage each other, just as brothers and sisters would. It is not unusual for churches to gather for things such as picnics and concerts as opportunities to celebrate their life of faith as part of God's family. The gatherings include people from all ages and stages of life.

All the functions, duties, privileges, and obligations that human families share also are present in the Christian family of faith. Christians are instructed to love and respect each other, as Christ does the church. In keeping with this idea, many believers call one another "brother" or "sister" as a reminder that they all are part of one spiritual family. Christians congregate together as family to share what they have and to teach, support, and encourage other believers. As in all families, Christians sometimes have disagreements. However, when problems do occur between Christians, Scripture instructs them to seek out the guidance of the wisest and most spiritually mature believers for help. These wise leaders of the church are *elders,* and they are often called upon to mediate disputes, much like a mother or father does in a family. In these situations, Christians are called to willingly forgive one another. Forgiveness is an important church practice because it keeps the body of Christ working together in harmony, and it reminds all believers that Christians forgive because God has forgiven them. When they do this, it shows respect and honor for God, who willingly offers forgiveness to all human beings who ask.

Types and Families of Christian Churches

The experience of worship has been passed from one generation to the next, and the Christian communities of today often
incorporate the symbols, creeds, rituals, and practices handed
down from the first believers. Although specific practices vary
from congregation to congregation, there is only one Christian religion. With respect to Christian worship, there are two
general types of services: formal and informal. Formal services
favor more structured worship, with greater focus on liturgy,
the public rites and rituals of the Christian faith. Churches following this pattern use printed prayers and group readings, and
they celebrate Holy Communion every Sunday. Churches with
this kind of service — often Catholic, Orthodox, Lutheran, or
Anglican — sometimes are called "liturgical" churches.

Informal services have less structured and more spontaneous
worship, with little emphasis given to liturgy. Formal services
often have older, more traditional music, played on traditional church instruments such as organ or piano. Informal
services often favor more modern music, played on guitars,
drums, and electronic instruments. Members of the congregation may express themselves in extemporaneous ways such as
clapping hands, shouting, or dancing. These services sometimes
are called "contemporary worship."

Although these types of worship can be found in almost
any denomination, one or the other (liturgical or contemporary) tends to predominate in a given denomination. As we
mentioned in chapter 1, the Christian religion generally is expressed in three traditions: Catholic, Orthodox, and Protestant.
Broadly speaking, the more formal services take place in Catholic and Orthodox churches, but they also are found in some
Protestant churches that are strongly influenced by them. Protestant churches generally place more emphasis on preaching,
and usually have more informal worship. These things are not

Major Protestant Churches

Lutheran

Calvinist (includes Reformed and
    Presbyterian)

Anabaptist (includes Amish and Mennonites)

Baptist and Congregational

Anglican (includes Episcopalian and the
    Church of England)

Wesleyan (includes Methodist, Holiness, and
    Salvation Army)

Independent and Nondenominational

Pentecostal

universal, however. It is possible to go on Sunday morning to a very formal liturgical service, including incense and bells, in an *Episcopalian* church, and then to attend on Sunday evening a very informal "folk *Mass*," with guitars and contemporary music, at a Roman Catholic church. These variations reflect the rich cultural and theological heritage of Christianity, and they witness to the creative nature of worship.

The names given to church leaders also differ, depending on tradition. As we have already noted, local leaders may be called pastors, priests, or elders. Most churches will also have leadership above the local pastor. Traditionally, a leader called a *"bishop"* supervises local pastors and the affairs of several churches within a particular area. The bishop of an important or large city may be called an "archbishop." The Eastern Orthodox tradition also appoints leaders above bishops. This church official is called a "metropolitan," or for very old and important cities, a *"patriarch."* There are several independent Eastern Orthodox churches, each with its own leader or patriarch. The most respected and important patriarch is the ecumenical patriarch of Constantinople, which is now modern Istanbul. He is the symbolic spiritual leader of Orthodoxy.

In the Roman Catholic tradition, the leader of the entire Catholic Church is called the *"pope"* (addressed as "Holy Father"). He is the supreme pastor of the church, but he appoints special advisors who bear the title "cardinal." When a pope dies, the cardinals elect his successor, usually from within their number. The pope lives in the Vatican, a small city-state in the middle of Rome, and is one of the world's best-known and most influential religious leaders.

Questions for Further Reflection

1. The church is described in Scripture as a family and as a body. What do these analogies tell you about what it means to be a Christian?

2. If you were going to attend a worship service, would you prefer a church with a formal or an informal style of worship? Why?

3. Is there a particular church (denomination) that you are most familiar with? What do you like most about this particular church, and why?

4. Many theologians have argued that some kind of worship is crucial to a meaningful human life. Do you agree or disagree? Why?

Chapter 4

Who Is Jesus?

The life and teachings of Jesus of Nazareth stand at the heart of the Christian faith. Christians believe that he is the Christ, meaning the Messiah or the Anointed One, the savior who was promised by God. Jesus Christ, who sacrificed himself on the cross in order to free his followers from the power of evil, *sin,* and death, is central to Christian worship. As we have already seen, sacred time and sacred space are organized around his life, death, and resurrection. The church's year is a kind of extended meditation on Jesus. Likewise, the course of Western civilization has been shaped by Jesus Christ and by the religion that bears his name. Despite this, little is known about the life of Jesus prior to the beginning of his ministry, at the age of thirty.

What we do know about Jesus' life comes primarily from the Bible, especially the first four books of the New Testament. These books tell the story of Jesus, and are called "Gospels," a term derived from an old word meaning "good news." From his birth in humble surroundings to his death by crucifixion under the Romans, Jesus lived among the common people. He lived a life surrounded by all the joys and sorrows that are part of being human; he knew what it felt like to be hungry, cold, and tired, and he also knew what it felt like to celebrate and dance and to hold the hand of a small child.

Jesus and His People,
the Jews

Based upon modern calculations, it appears that Jesus was born about 4 B.C. (which means, ironically, four years "before Christ" on the modern Western calendar). The Gospel of Luke provides the best-known account of the birth of Jesus, locating the event during the reign of the Roman emperor Caesar Augustus (Luke 2:1). Jesus was born in Bethlehem, but his parents were from Nazareth, in Galilee. Thus, he also is known as Jesus of Nazareth. From this information we know that Jesus spent much of his life in a rural, "small town" area of Palestine. As the firstborn son in his family, Jesus likely worked alongside his father, Joseph, in the carpentry trade (Matthew 13:55; Mark 6:3). The Bible also shows that Jesus had brothers and sisters (Mark 3:32), and that some of his brothers later came to accept him as the Messiah (Acts 1:14). He and his family of origin were Jews, and the Bible makes it clear that he practiced and understood *Judaism,* the faith of his people.

Father Abraham

The Jewish people, also called Hebrews, trace their heritage and their religion back to Abraham and Sarah. According to the Hebrew Scriptures, the patriarch Abraham was chosen by God to be the father of a great people, with descendants too numerous to count. He lived almost two thousand years before Christ (about 1800 B.C.), and his son Isaac and grandson Jacob are the ancestors of the Jewish people.

During the time of Jesus there were four main types of Judaism. Jews at this time lived not only in Palestine, but also throughout the Roman Empire. Still, the spiritual center was in Jerusalem, the capital city of Judea. The closest of these groups to the religion of Jesus himself were the **Pharisees.** This group was a conservative movement, with strength in the countryside rather than in the cities. They were concerned to protect the unique identity of Hebrew faith and Jewish laws in the face of a dominant Greek and Roman culture. In the cities, the **Sadducees** were more in favor of collaboration with the Roman government and Greek culture. Greek culture (also called "Hellenistic") was highly prized by many people of that day, including Jews and Romans. The more Hellenistic Sadducees were typical of the urban, ruling class in Judea (which was a part of the Roman Empire).

At the other end of the spectrum from the Sadducees, the **Essenes** were even more **separatist** than the Pharisees. They rejected the temple in Jerusalem and all **pagan** (non-Jewish) culture. The most zealous of them lived apart from pagans and other Jews in desert communities. They believed that the Messiah would come very soon and begin the war of the children of light (Jews who agreed with Essene teachings) against the children of darkness (pagans and Jews who disagreed with them). The Essenes wrote the Dead Sea Scrolls at Qumran, one of the most important and famous archeological finds of the twentieth century. The **Zealots** were another extremist group. They sought to begin the battle against Roman oppression as soon as possible. They assassinated Roman officials and military leaders, and instigated immediate revolt. They also believed that the Messiah would come soon to help them. When you read the Gospels, remember that many of the people listening to Jesus came from one of the Jewish groups discussed here.

The work and teaching of Jesus took place against the background of Jewish faith in his own day, and it was understood

The Dead Sea Scrolls

In 1947 and for years after, hundreds of very old scrolls (rolled-up books) have come from the Dead Sea region in Palestine. The main location where these scrolls were found is Qumran, just south of Jericho, in several caves. These texts in Hebrew and Aramaic provide a very important window into the biblical world from about 250 B.C. to A.D. 70. They contain the oldest texts of the Hebrew Bible, commentaries on the Bible, community rules, prayers, and other religious texts from the Essene community. Among the most important scrolls are *The Manual of Discipline,* the *Damascus Covenant,* the *Temple Scroll,* the *War Scroll,* and the *Thanksgiving Hymns.* These precious documents are now housed in the Rockefeller and Israel Museums in Jerusalem.

against the backdrop of Roman occupation and oppression. He came from a humble, working-class family in the outback region of Palestine. Galilee was rather far from the capital, Jerusalem, and had the reputation of being a backwater village. Jesus came from peasant stock in an obscure part of the Roman Empire. It is also true that he is the single most important individual in Western history; his life and teachings have had a greater impact in the West than any other individual. But what did Jesus do that was worthy of such a vast following, or even the comparatively small following that he had during his own lifetime? To help us understand, we look at some of the significant events in the life of Jesus Christ. The most important events in his life are (1) the beginning of his ministry; (2) his teaching in Galilee and Judea; (3) his conflict with Jewish leaders, especially his cleansing of the Jerusalem temple; (4) his arrest, trial, and execution; and (5) his resurrection. We will look at each of these in turn.

The Beginning of His Ministry

We know little of Jesus' upbringing in Nazareth. His excellent knowledge of the Bible would suggest that he came from a devout Jewish home. When he was about thirty years old, Jesus was baptized by his cousin John the Baptist in the river Jordan (Luke 3:23). He called some of John's disciples to join him in wandering from town to town, teaching about God and Scripture. Jesus thus was a kind of country *rabbi*, a Jewish teacher and preacher, but he did not go to school in Jerusalem as the official rabbis did. He went from village to village, teaching the common people and performing miracles. He seems to have focused his early work on the area around Capernaum on the Sea of Galilee.

The women and men who follow Jesus are called *disciples*. Out of all the women and men who followed Jesus and heard his teachings gladly, he selected twelve men to be his *apostles* (Mark 3:13–19). The word "apostle" comes from a Greek word meaning "one who is sent." These men were his closest followers; they traveled, ate, and slept where he did. The Gospels portray them as giving up their work and families to follow and live with Jesus.

Jesus never married, which was quite unusual for a rabbi, and this may be the reason he chose only men to be his closest companions. Although Jesus chose only men to be his twelve apostles, he did have women disciples (Luke 8:1–3), which was highly unusual for his day. That Jesus chose twelve apostles is significant in itself. Israel was, by tradition, founded by twelve brothers, all the sons of Jacob (Genesis 49:28). That Jesus appointed twelve apostles suggests that he sought to create a new Israel — that is, a new people of God — beginning with his own disciples. Knowing exactly what Jesus thought of himself, however, is often rather difficult.

Although Jesus accepted the title "Messiah" in some sense of the word (John 4:25–26; Matthew 16:13–20), he rejected the political overtones that accompanied it (John 18:36; cf. Luke 23:2). Jesus did not want to be seen as a Zealot, and was not interested in political revolution. For this reason, he told others not to broadcast the fact that he was the Messiah or Christ, the Anointed One of God (Mark 8:29–30; Matthew 16:20). Instead of using well-worn labels from other groups, Jesus used the term "Son of Man" to describe God's servant, the one who would come to restore Israel. This allowed him to fill the term with his own meaning rather than accepting one shaped by the expectations of others. Although the Son of Man was someone to come in the future (Mark 13:26), Jesus may have understood himself to be this Son of Man too. Like most interesting things about the Bible, these points are debated by modern scholars.

His Teaching

A central theme of the teaching of Jesus was the kingdom of God (in Matthew's Gospel, it is called the kingdom of heaven). Mark's Gospel reports that after his baptism by John, "Jesus came to Galilee, proclaiming the gospel of God, and saying, 'The time is fulfilled, and the kingdom of God is at hand; repent and believe in the gospel' " (Mark 1:14–15). The good news of the *gospel* is that God's forgiveness is available to all those who repent — that is, turn away from sin — and turn to God. The idea of God as "king" means that God is the ultimate ruler, one who establishes law and justice and seeks to have a people who are obedient. The kingdom of God, in Jesus' preaching, stands for at least three things: (1) the power and presence of God in those who accept God as sovereign ruler; (2) the community of all those in heaven and on earth who believe and obey God; and (3) the future reign of God over all the earth, when sin and evil will be destroyed. This third meaning is associated with the future coming of the Son of Man (see in the Old Testament, Daniel 7:13–14).

In teaching about the kingdom, Jesus used parables, which are stories with an important message, drawn from everyday life in Galilee. By telling parables, Jesus' message could reach the uneducated masses of ordinary people. One example of a famous parable by Jesus is the story of the Good Samaritan:

> Just then a lawyer stood up to test Jesus. "Teacher," he said, "what must I do to inherit eternal life?" He said to him, "What is written in the law? What do you read there?" He answered, "You shall love the Lord your God with all your heart, and with all your soul, and with all your strength, and with all your mind; and your neighbor as yourself." And he said to him, "You have given the right answer; do this, and you will live."
>
> But wanting to justify himself, he asked Jesus, "And who is my neighbor?" Jesus replied, "A man was going down from Jerusalem to Jericho, and fell into the hands of robbers, who stripped him, beat him, and went away, leaving him half dead. Now by chance a priest was going down that road; and when he saw him, he passed by on the other side. So likewise a Levite, when he came to the place and saw him, passed by on the other side. But a Samaritan while traveling came near him; and when he saw him, he was moved with pity. He went to him and bandaged his wounds, having poured oil and wine on them. Then he put him on his own animal, brought him to an inn, and took care of him. The next day he took

out two denarii, gave them to the innkeeper, and said, 'Take care of him; and when I come back, I will repay you whatever more you spend.'

Which of these three, do you think, was a neighbor to the man who fell into the hands of the robbers?" He said, "The one who showed him mercy." Jesus said to him, "Go and do likewise." (Luke 10:25–37)

The fact that the hero in this story is a Samaritan would have surprised the listeners in Jesus' day. Samaritans lived near the Jews, but were despised because of their mixed racial heritage and their religious practices. That Jesus chose a Samaritan, rather than honored Jewish leaders such as Levites and priests, is important. He sought in all of his teaching and ministry to overcome the hurtful barriers and prejudices that divided people from each other. Throughout his ministry, Jesus reached out to the outsiders and the hated underclass: prostitutes, tax collectors, Samaritans, lepers, the poor, and the blind. Christians believe that through his own actions, Jesus demonstrated that the kingdom of God is open to all people.

As the parable of the Good Samaritan makes clear, Jesus' teachings about the kingdom are not simply about God's future rule over all the earth. The kingdom begins in his own ministry (see, e.g., Matthew 12:28), and it will change the lives of those who seek to enter into it. The greatest commandment is to love God, but the second greatest is to love your neighbor as yourself. This, of course, is what the parable of the Good Samaritan is all about. But this ethic of love is not a romantic emotion; rather, it is a call for justice, and it demands sacrifice on the part of those who would follow Jesus in the kingdom of God.

Jesus roundly condemned those who misled or oppressed the people (see Matthew 23:1–36), and his close association with the poor and those rejected by society led many to criticize him. Jesus said,

Woe to you who are rich, for you have received your consolation. Woe to you who are full now, for you will be hungry. Woe to you who are laughing now, for you will mourn and weep. Woe to you when all speak well of you, for that is what their ancestors did to the false prophets. (Luke 6:24–26)

He called upon his followers to give sacrificially to others, even to their enemies:

I say to you that listen, Love your enemies, do good to those who hate you, bless those who curse you, pray for those who abuse you. If anyone strikes you on the cheek, offer the other also; and from anyone who takes away your coat do not withhold even your shirt. Give to everyone who begs from you; and if anyone takes away your goods, do not ask for them again. Do to others as you would have them do to you. (Luke 6:27–31)

Following Jesus meant denying oneself for the sake of others. Many scholars today believe that the radical teachings and actions of Jesus, which led him into conflict with the powerful leaders of his day, also led to his death on a cross.

His Conflict with Jewish Leaders

Given his teaching and ethics, it seems inevitable that Jesus would come into conflict with other Jewish leaders. Verbal conflict among the various Jewish groups was common in his day. In a relatively short time, Jesus became a leader with a public profile, in part because of his miracles. He appealed to the poor and the outcast, who seem to have followed him gladly. He soon came into conflict with the leaders of his day, and with other Jewish teachers. We often find Jesus condemning the Pharisees, for example, who were close to him in their teachings

and practices. Jesus thought that they emphasized the letter of
the law too heavily (see, e.g., Matthew 15:1–20), especially as
their teaching was experienced by the country poor and ordinary folk. Jesus had few dealings with Sadducees, since he was
from the rural area of Galilee. Remember that the Sadducees
included many of the chief collaborators with Rome, and their
strength was in the cities. The Gospels do record one debate
that he had with them, however. It was about the resurrection
(Mark 12:18–27). As for the Zealots, the teachings of Jesus
would have been unacceptable to them. The ethical teachings
of Jesus about peace, forgiveness, and paying taxes to Caesar
were not at all in line with the party of the Zealots. Their way
of life was too warlike and violent.

John the Baptist, Jesus' cousin, probably was close to the Essenes in practice and belief. Although Jesus was close to John
the Baptist in many ways, he understood religious life and practice differently. We can see some indication of these differences
in a response by Jesus to those who opposed both John the
Baptist and himself:

> But to what will I compare this generation? It is like chil-
> dren sitting in the marketplaces and calling to one another,
> "We played the flute for you, and you did not dance; we
> wailed, and you did not mourn." For John came neither
> eating nor drinking, and they say, "He has a demon";
> the Son of Man came eating and drinking, and they say,
> "Look, a glutton and a drunkard, a friend of tax collectors
> and sinners!" (Matthew 11:16–19)

The critics of Jesus saw him as a glutton, a drunkard, and a friend
of tax collectors and sinners. Although Jesus greatly admired John
the Baptist, he did not follow his strict religious practices. Jesus
enjoyed meals with those whom others would despise.

The major event that brought Jesus into conflict with the
political leadership of Israel was his cleansing of the temple

in Jerusalem. This occurred after three years of ministry in Galilee and Judea, when Jesus made a final trip to Jerusalem. It happened during the most important Jewish religious festival, Passover. The many merchants making money off of the temple and the sacrifices of the people angered Jesus. He tipped over the tables of the money changers, and drove those selling animals for sacrifice out of the temple area (Mark 11:15–16). But by opposing the way the temple sacrifices were being run, he angered the chief priests of Israel. Mark narrates that they "began seeking a way to destroy him" (Mark 11:18). Although Jesus already had many opponents, this major public display during the largest festival of the year brought opposition to him to a head. He had, in effect, placed himself above the chief priests as if he were a new kind of Moses.

His Arrest, Trial, and Execution

After sharing a last Passover meal with his disciples, Jesus went off to pray. He was betrayed by one of his own from within the inner circle of the twelve apostles, Judas Iscariot. After a hasty sham trial, the Jewish leaders handed Jesus over to the Roman governor, Pontius Pilate. Although Pilate was reluctant to execute a man for no apparent reason, in order to pacify the riotous crowds he handed Jesus over to be crucified. In crucifixion, a person was nailed to a wooden cross and left hanging there until dead, usually a long and painful process of suffering. Normally, those crucified had the nature of their crime inscribed on a placard affixed to the cross, above their head. Pilate had "The King of the Jews" written there for Jesus, even though John reports that the chief priests objected to this (they thought that it should read, "He claimed to be King of the Jews") (John 19:19–22). Jesus died on a Friday afternoon, on the eve of the day of the Passover.

As a poor man, Jesus had no burial place or tomb. A prominent man sympathetic to Jesus, Joseph of Arimathea, donated his own tomb as a place for Jesus to be buried.

His Resurrection

Jesus died on a Friday afternoon, not long before sundown, which was the beginning of the *Sabbath,* a Jewish day of worship on which no work could be done (the Sabbath begins each Friday night at sundown and lasts until Saturday night). Because it was a Sabbath, the usual Jewish rituals surrounding death were not fully performed on Jesus. So on Sunday morning, as soon as it was light (after Saturday night and the end of the Sabbath), some of Jesus' women disciples came to his tomb to finish burying him properly. They found the tomb empty.

Christians believe that the burial tomb was empty because God transformed Jesus' body, bringing him from death into eternal life. Jesus came back to life with a renewed body, never to die again, and promised his followers that they too would be resurrected from the dead when he returned in the future (John 11:25–27). Some scholars have argued that such a thing could not have happened. However, what historians do agree upon is that a number of Jesus' disciples claimed to have seen him resurrected from the dead. He had entered into a new, eternal life, but still had a (transformed) human body. According to Luke, Jesus then was carried up to heaven, an event known as the *ascension* (Luke 24:51). Christians believe that Jesus is alive, and that he will come again in the future.

What Christians Believe about Jesus

With the obvious exception of the resurrection and the ascension, much of the story of Jesus can be accepted by historical

The Christian Gospels

Although the Gospels themselves do not tell us who wrote them, tradition has named the authors as Matthew, Mark, Luke, and John. Like all Bible books, the Gospels later were divided into chapters and verses, and now are cited by that method (e.g., in John 1:1, we read, "In the beginning was the Word, and the Word was with God, and the Word was God"). In addition to these works, there are later Gospels, such as the Gospel of Thomas and the Gospel of Peter, which are not included in the New Testament. They are part of what we call the Apocrypha. The word "apocrypha" comes from a Greek word meaning "hidden," now used in the sense of "closed out" of the Bible. These Gospels are viewed as "pseudepigrapha," from a Greek word meaning "falsely inscribed" (i.e., not written by the author named in the book), and are considered to be less reliable than the four biblical Gospels for accurate knowledge about Jesus.

scholars whether they are Christian or not. The disciples went further than this basic story. Based on their own experience of Jesus, and the memories of his deeds and words, the earliest church came to believe that Jesus was more than just a great prophet or even the Messiah. They came to believe that God was present and at work in a unique way in Jesus Christ. The deposit of these beliefs is found in the New Testament.

After the Gospels, the New Testament consists of the book of Acts (the Acts of the Apostles), which is a sequel to the Gospel of Luke; a number of letters from apostles such as Peter, Paul, and John; and a final book, Revelation (also known as the Apocalypse). To understand the Christian religion, we will look at some of the beliefs that early Christians held regarding Jesus.

First, you should remember that all of the earliest Christians were Jews. They called their Jewish sect "the Way," and it was only in Antioch (outside Israel) that others called them Christians. Already the small Jewish sect was growing beyond Israel.

Members of this early movement believed, first of all, that Jesus was the true Messiah of Israel (the Christ), as foretold in the Hebrew Scriptures. One example of this early conclusion by the Christians is in a sermon by Peter, found in the second chapter of Acts. There, Peter, one of the most important of the twelve apostles, explains to his fellow Israelites that Jesus is the true Messiah, and that the psalms had predicted his resurrection. "This Jesus God raised up, and of that we are all witnesses.... Therefore let the entire house of Israel know with certainty that God has made him both Lord and Messiah, this Jesus whom you crucified" (Acts 2:32, 36).

Belief in the resurrection was key to the earliest Christians' acceptance of Jesus as Christ or Messiah. They also called him the "Son of God," a term that probably means very much the same thing, but had more meaning for non-Jews. For example, in his important letter to the Romans, the apostle Paul (not one of the original twelve) writes that he is sent by Jesus to teach "the gospel concerning his [God's] Son, who was descended from David according to the flesh and was declared to be Son of God with power according to the Spirit of holiness by resurrection from the dead" (Romans 1:3–4). Thus, the resurrection was a central event in the formation of *Christology* in the early church.

Another important element in the Christology of the early church was the crucifixion — the cross of Christ. In the cross, God offered atonement, a means of forgiveness, for the sins of the whole world. Paul, again in his letter to the Romans, declares, "God put forward [Jesus] as a sacrifice of atonement by his blood, effective through faith" (Romans 3:25). Many religions throughout history have made sacrifices to the gods, very often blood sacrifices. In the eyes of the early Christians, God reversed this process. God provided the sacrifice, in Jesus Christ, for the sins of all people.

The apostle Paul was also committed to Jesus' message that the good news of God's love and forgiveness was for all humankind. In particular, Paul argued that in Christ, the usual divisions and distinctions of race and religion had been overcome. All believers are one in Christ. The old division between Jews and *Gentiles* (non-Jew) was now gone. Since Christ has become savior for the whole world, Jews and Gentiles alike are able to be reconciled with God (see Romans 9–11). Likewise, the difference between slaves and free people, or between men and women, is of no significance for the new community of the Messiah (Galatians 3:28). Through Christ, God was reconciling the whole world to himself (2 Corinthians 5:19).

The logic of this argument about how God has worked through Jesus led the church to an astounding conclusion. Jesus Christ was in some way divine, God's own special agent living a human life. The opening of the great letter to the Hebrews declares that Jesus is the Son of God. "He is the reflection of God's glory and the exact imprint of God's very being, and he sustains all things by his powerful word" (Hebrews 1:3). The beautiful and renowned beginning of the Gospel of John says, "In the beginning was the Word, and the Word was with God, and the Word was God.... And the Word became flesh and lived among us, and we have seen his glory, the glory of the Father's only Son, full of grace and truth" (John 1:1, 14). And in a long passage in praise of Jesus, Paul writes in his letter to the Colossians, "He is the image of the invisible God, the firstborn of all creation.... For in him all the fullness of God was pleased to dwell" (Colossians 1:15, 19). The New Testament does not explain these poetic expressions of the divinity of Jesus. In fact, centuries passed before the church would understand fully who Jesus was in relationship to God. After hundreds of years of debate, prayer, and discussion, the church came to believe that Jesus was both fully human *and* fully divine. How this can be so, however, has long been a major source of theological discussion in the church.

So just who was Jesus of Nazareth? We know that he actually lived, that he had followers who took his teachings seriously, and that the entire world has been shaped by him and his followers. Yet the question of Jesus' identity as the Christ cannot be answered "objectively" or in a neutral fashion. Any response to this question will always involve, to some degree, the faith of the one who seeks to know the truth. A purely scientific or scholarly answer to the question of faith is not possible. The nature of Christian claims does not allow it. Any authentic encounter with Jesus will demand a searching of one's most basic beliefs. What is the meaning of life? Is there really a God? Are miracles possible? Was Jesus a great Jewish prophet, or was he something more? Did he really rise from the dead, as the earliest Christians proclaimed? These demanding questions require a combination of faith and reason, of our rational and emotional sides. Christians believe that faith takes the work of God in our minds, and the human response of trust.

However one answers the basic question, "Who was Jesus?" one fact remains: this obscure Jewish carpenter from a tiny village in the middle of nowhere lived the single most influential life in all of history. He began a worldwide movement that is still gaining ground around the globe more than two thousand years after he lived, taught, died, and (Christians believe) rose from the dead.

Questions for Further Reflection

1. Why did early followers of Jesus call him the "Christ"?
2. What was Jesus' relationship to the Jewish religion and Scriptures of his day?
3. Why did Jesus use parables for his teaching?
4. Do you believe the Gospel accounts of Jesus' resurrection? Why or why not?

Chapter 5

The Bible — The Christian Book

As we have seen, what Christians understand about Jesus comes in part from their holy book, the Bible. The word "Bible" comes from a Latin word meaning "books." This "book of books" is a collection of ancient writings sacred to the faith. To Christians, these sacred Scriptures are essential for a full knowledge of God, God's work in history, and the path to human *salvation.* Here, Christians see a record of God's relationship with humankind, expressed as historical narrative, poetry, wise sayings, and prophecy about what God will do in the future. Because they believe that this book is God's unique revelation, Christians give it special honor and respect as a source of divine authority in their lives. Believers have always read and reflected upon this holy text in Christian worship and teaching. In this they follow Jesus Christ, who himself studied and taught from many of these sacred writings. In this chapter, we will give you an introduction to the Christian holy book, the Bible. We first will discuss the Old Testament, also known as the Hebrew Bible. From there we will look to the New Testament, and then conclude with an explanation of Bible translations.

Old Testament and Hebrew Bible

The Old Testament, written in Hebrew, is the Bible of the Jews. They divide the Hebrew Bible into three parts: the Torah, the

---

The Bible: Chapter and Verse

The books of the Bible were divided long ago into numbered chapters. Chapters were then divided up into verses, which were also numbered. Modern Bibles still use this system of citation. To find a verse in the Bible, you must know three things: the name of the book, the number of the chapter, and the number of the verse. For example, if you were trying to find Matthew 2:1, you would go to the book of Matthew, the second chapter, and the first verse.

Prophets, and the Writings. The Torah, or Law, is also known as the Books of Moses, and the Pentateuch. The word "Pentateuch" comes from a Greek word meaning "five vessels," because it is a group of five books. These books are Genesis, Exodus, Leviticus, Numbers, and Deuteronomy. The first of these, Genesis, contains the oldest stories. It begins with a simple story of the creation of the world. In the story, God commands the heaven and earth into existence, and here God places the first humans, Adam and Eve. Although these new beings were created for a loving relationship with God, the story tells us that human beings rejected God's love. Christians refer to this human rebellion as the "fall," because here humanity falls out of relationship with God.

These accounts, along with others in the first eleven chapters of Genesis, are prehistorical sagas. They are extremely old stories, handed down orally from a time before historical records were kept. These include stories such as Noah's ark and the flood, the Tower of Babel, and other events from the misty past.

The Septuagint

True to its name, the Old Testament is very old indeed. These are the holy writings of the Jews in ancient Israel, and were originally written in Hebrew, the language of the Jews. However, long before the time of Christ's birth, the Jewish people had been dispersed throughout the Greco-Roman world. Some communities could no longer understand the Hebrew language, and so Jewish scholars translated Hebrew scripture into Greek. Greek was the common language of the Greco-Roman world, and this translation allowed Greek-speaking Jews who did not know Hebrew to study their sacred writings. This Greek translation of the Hebrew Bible is known as the Septuagint.

In Genesis 12, we enter known history with the stories of Abraham and Sarah and their descendants. These are the stories of the patriarchs, the ancient ancestors of Israel. Other patriarchs (and matriarchs) are Isaac and Rebekah, Jacob (also called "Israel") and Rachel, and Jacob's twelve sons. The twelve sons of Jacob are the ancestors of the twelve tribes of Israel.

The rest of the Torah centers on the great Jewish leader Moses, the lawgiver. Exodus begins with the people in Egypt and tells the story of their liberation by God through Moses. Here we learn about Israel's miraculous exodus out of slavery and the gift of God's law at Mount Sinai. This law (in Hebrew, *torah*) begins with the Ten Commandments. Exodus ends, and Leviticus begins, when the glory of God moves from Sinai.

According to Scripture, God's presence continues with the Israelites on their journey through the desert. Because their travel through the desert lasts forty years, the people worship God in a tabernacle, a portable tent constructed for that purpose. The book of Leviticus focuses on laws relating to rituals, sacrifices, and worship in the tabernacle. These are concerned with the ritual holiness of the people. Later they are observed in the temple that was built in Jerusalem.

The book of Numbers continues the story of Israel. Here the people remain wanderers in the desert wilderness, led by Moses. They are searching for the Promised Land, territory in what is known as Palestine or the land of Israel. The last book of the Pentateuch is Deuteronomy. This is a retelling of the law. Its special focus is the people of God and their relationship with God through law and ritual. The law is a major part of this *covenant,* or special relationship, between God and his people. Deuteronomy also contains the Ten Commandments, as well as numerous other laws and stories that summarize the whole Pentateuch. Deuteronomy and the Torah end with the death of Moses and his final blessing on each of the tribes. The Torah is the guidebook for the covenant established between God and his people. It contains the basic teachings about ethics, ritual, and holiness in the law.

The next part of the Hebrew Bible, the Prophets, shows the way this covenant was obeyed, broken, and renewed in the history of Israel. Prophets are persons sent by God to bring a special message to the people. The job of the prophet often was to point out how the people had broken God's laws and to call them to repent. The Prophets, then, apply and extend the covenant revealed in the Torah to the Promised Land and the growth of Israel. The early Prophets, also known as the Former Prophets, are historical books. Joshua takes up the story after the death of Moses, just as the people begin to enter the Promised Land. Joshua continues the work of Moses as the people

Isaiah: Prophet of Israel

Isaiah was one of Israel's greatest prophets. He lived during the eighth century B.C. He preached against the sins of his people and proclaimed God's judgment on them for their actions. But his call was also for Israel to return to God. In chapter 55 of the book of Isaiah he writes:

> Seek the Lord while he may be found,
> call upon him while he is near;
> let the wicked forsake their way,
> and the unrighteous their thoughts;
> let them return to the Lord,
> that he may have mercy on them,
> and to our God,
> for he will abundantly pardon.

settle in Palestine. In Judges, we read of another group of early leaders of Israel, in a time before Israel had a king. The book of Judges tells of these leaders, who guided Israel through conflicts with neighboring tribes. Some of the better-known judges are Deborah, Gideon, and Samson. First and Second Samuel are the next books of this type, and they tell the story of the prophet Samuel and the coming of David, the great king of Israel. First and Second Kings continues the story of Israel after the death of David's son, King Solomon, when the land was divided into two kingdoms. The northern kingdom was called Israel, and the southern kingdom became known as Judah. This division between the two kingdoms was never healed.

One of the better-known groups of books in the Old Testament is the Latter Prophets, sometimes simply called the

Prophets. These books record the deeds and words of the great prophets of Israel, beginning in the eighth century B.C. The longest and best known of these books is Isaiah. While the prophet laments the pride and sin of Israel, especially the leaders in Jerusalem, the book also predicts a future age of justice and peace. Almost equal in length and reputation are the books of Jeremiah and Ezekiel. Jeremiah prophesied during the time when Jerusalem fell to its political enemies the Babylonians (586 B.C.). This was known as the exile, a time when many Jews were taken captive and forced to live in Babylon. Ezekiel lived during the exile, and his book contains God's message of judgment and hope to the captives. The book of Ezekiel is full of fantastic *apocalyptic* imagery — symbolic visions of God, heaven, and the future of the world.

Because of their length, Isaiah, Jeremiah, and Ezekiel are called the Major Prophets. The remaining works of Old Testament prophets are included in the Minor Prophets. These are comprised of twelve smaller books containing the prophecies from various times throughout the history of Israel. They are "minor" only in the sense of being short, not in the sense of being unimportant. The best known of these books are Hosea, Amos, and Jonah. The book of Hosea includes his prophecy against the northern kingdom, Israel. Hosea's marriage to an unfaithful wife is seen as a parallel to Israel's unfaithfulness to God. The love of God for his people, and his pain at their unfaithfulness to the covenant, is the key theme of the book. In the book of Amos, the prophet states God's case against Israel and the surrounding nations. The book of Jonah, on the other hand, tells more about a reluctant prophet than about a prophecy in itself. Here we learn the story of Jonah and of his ill-fated attempt to disobey God.

The Writings are the latest part of the Hebrew Bible. They contain the Israelites' response to the revelation of God in law and prophecy. Sometimes these are separated into poetic books

The Twenty-third Psalm

The Lord is my shepherd, I shall not want.
He makes me lie down in green pastures;
he leads me beside still waters;
he restores my soul.
He leads me in right paths for his name's
    sake.
Even though I walk through the darkest
    valley,
I fear no evil; for you are with me;
your rod and your staff — they comfort me.
You prepare a table before me in the
    presence of my enemies;
you anoint my head with oil; my cup
    overflows.
Surely goodness and mercy shall follow me
    all the days of my life,
and I shall dwell in the house of the Lord my
    whole life long.

and wisdom books. The best known of the Writings, and in many ways most loved, is the book of Psalms. Here we read the hymns of ancient Israel, songs to God collected over many generations. Psalms are reflections upon God and life, and are a rich deposit for the life of prayer. Among the books of wisdom in the Writings we find Proverbs, which contains short sayings about how to live a successful life with God and in the world. The book of Job also is a wisdom book. It tells the story of a righteous man who is afflicted with pain and suffering. Faithfulness to God, even in the midst of suffering, is the main theme of the book. One of the Writings is known by three titles: the Song of Songs, Canticles, or Song of Solomon. It is a love poem.

The book of Ruth tells the story of a young woman who leaves her people to join Israel during the time of the judges. She is one of the ancestors of King David. Lamentations is a poem expressing grief over the fall of Jerusalem. Ecclesiastes, also known as Qoheleth, is a wisdom book that points out the foolishness of a life lived for pleasure, power, and fame. It calls instead for a simple life of service to God. Esther tells the story of Queen Esther, a Jewish woman who lived during the exile. She risked her own safety to help save her people from persecution and death. The book of Daniel contains prophecies, stories, and visions and dreams from a Jewish leader who served the rulers of Persia during the exile. Persia conquered Babylon in 539 B.C. and took over its empire. Like Ezekiel, Daniel has some apocalyptic parts.

Ezra and Nehemiah are historical books that take place during the time of the Persian Empire. Ezra was a scribe and priest who lived during the return of Israel from exile back to Jerusalem. Nehemiah was a Persian court official and a leader of the Jews who lived and worked at the same time as Ezra. The book of Nehemiah is a kind of diary of his activities, and tells of rebuilding Jerusalem and the temple. Finally, First and Second Chronicles retell the history of Israel from Abraham, the father of Israel, to the exile. It begins with a genealogy of Israel, stretching back to Adam and Eve. This retelling is interpreted in light of the exile and the return, and a hope for the rebuilding of the temple. This ends the Hebrew Bible. For many Christians, however, it does not end the Old Testament, as we will see.

The Old Testament Canon

A *canon* is a kind of list. When used in regard to the Bible, the word "canon" refers to a list of books that are considered to be holy; they are books that speak with the authority of God's

The Greek Septuagint

The word "Septuagint" comes from a Latin word for the number seventy and is abbreviated by the symbol "LXX," the Roman numeral for seventy. This comes from an ancient tradition that seventy-two scholars in Egypt translated the Hebrew Bible into Greek in seventy-two days. The Septuagint also contains some books that were not written in Hebrew but still are accepted by some parts of the church as being biblical. These Greek works are known as the Deutero-canonical Books or the Old Testament Apocrypha.

Word. Early Christians, many of whom were also Jews, spoke Greek and used the Septuagint, the Greek translation of the Hebrew Bible. This Greek Old Testament (which contains more books than does the Hebrew Bible) became a standard part of Christian worship in both the East and the West for well over a thousand years. The Greek translation was also incorporated into St. Jerome's fifth-century Vulgate, a Latin translation of the Bible that eventually became official Holy Scripture for the Roman Catholic Church. It was the standard Western Bible until the sixteenth century.

Despite the general acceptance of the Septuagint within the Christian church, disputes eventually arose over which books from the Septuagint belonged in the Old Testament canon. In the West, the matter of the Old Testament canon was opened amid the turbulence and upheaval of the Protestant *Reformation* in the sixteenth century. The Reformation, with its

Why the Septuagint?

Jesus was a Jew and was recognized for his ability to understand and explain the Hebrew Scriptures. Since Christianity began as a religious movement among Jews, the Scripture read by the early Christians was the Hebrew Bible. However, as the Christian faith spread out from Israel across the Roman Empire, most new followers of Jesus Christ were unfamiliar with Hebrew language and customs. Since few believers could understand Hebrew, but almost all could understand Greek, the Septuagint became the version most Christians studied. The Septuagint thus became the first part of the Christian Bible.

intense focus upon Christian Scripture, brought the whole question of the canon into the center of sixteenth-century religious and political debate. The disagreement over the Old Testament canon turned on the question of what was the "original" Bible. Protestants, such as the German reformer Martin Luther, insisted that the Hebrew Bible was original. They argued that only works written in Hebrew were fully God's Word. The debate revolved around a group of fifteen texts not originally written in Hebrew.

These works, known to Catholics as the Deuterocanonical Books and to Protestants as the Apocrypha, were written much later than the undisputed canonical books in the Hebrew Bible. Thus, when Martin Luther translated the Bible into German, he declared that the later books did not have the full authority of Scripture, although he still included the disputed books in his translation. This understanding, shared by earlier biblical scholars such as St. Jerome, saw the Deuterocanonical Books as valuable for the edification of the church but not authoritative in matters of doctrine. This meant that the books have great spiritual value for Christian readers but should not be used as the basis for church teachings. Luther's position became the standard for Protestants, but it was rejected by the Catholic Church. At the *Council of Trent* in 1546, the Catholic Church affirmed all books included in the Latin Vulgate as canonical.

In the Greek-speaking East, tradition favored the books of the Septuagint. No official canon of the Old Testament would be made until the Synod of Jerusalem in 1672. This clearly was a response to the Catholic canon in the Council of Trent. At the Synod of Jerusalem, the Orthodox accepted all Old Testament books in the Septuagint. Because of the small differences between the Latin Vulgate and the Greek Bible (Septuagint), the Orthodox have a slightly different canon than do the Catholics.

The Deuterocanonical Books

The Old Testament Apocrypha, or Deuterocanonical Books, span the period between the Hebrew Bible and the New Testament. The book of 1 Esdras is about Ezra ("Esdras," in Greek), and is a historical retelling of his work. There is also a book called 2 Esdras, which is not canonical. It contains apocalyptic visions attributed to Ezra. The book of Tobit tells the story of Tobit and Tobias. Tobit is a righteous man whose good deeds bring unjust suffering. Tobias journeys from Jerusalem to Nineveh to help him. The book contains many miraculous stories, including the healing of Tobit's blindness. The book of Judith is the story of a righteous Jewish woman who lures the general of a pagan army to his death, saving her hometown from

Deuterocanonical Books	
Greek (Orthodox)	*Latin (Catholic)*
1 Esdras	
Tobit	Tobit
Judith	Judith
Additions to Esther	Additions to Esther
Wisdom of Solomon	Wisdom of Solomon
Sirach (Ecclesiasticus)	Sirach (Ecclesiasticus)
Baruch (including the Letter of Jeremiah)	Letter of Jeremiah (in Jeremiah)
	Baruch
Additions to Daniel	Additions to Daniel
Prayer of Manasseh	
1–3 Maccabees	1–2 Maccabees

capture. The Additions to Esther includes a few passages found only in the Greek version of the book of Esther. Sirach (also known as Ecclesiasticus) and the Wisdom of Solomon are excellent examples of later Jewish wisdom literature. They show the influence of Greek philosophy upon Jewish thought. Baruch is a book supposedly written by the secretary and friend of Jeremiah. It tells more of Baruch and the exile in Babylon. It also contains some wisdom literature in its second part. The Letter of Jeremiah sometimes is included in the book of Baruch. It is a long sermon against idolatry, which very likely did not come from Jeremiah. The Additions to Daniel contains portions of the book of Daniel found only in the Greek version. These portions have been given separate titles: The Prayer of Azariah and the Song of the Three Young Men; Susanna; and Bel and the Dragon.

Finally, the books of 1 and 2 Maccabees tell the story of Israel after the coming of the Greeks. Central to this story is the pollution of the Jerusalem temple by the Greek ruler Antiochus IV, about 167 B.C. Antiochus wanted to dedicate the temple to the pagan god Zeus, and he outlawed Jewish religious practice, laws, and customs. This sparked a rebellion led by the priest Mattathias and his sons, most notably Judas Maccabeus. The Jews recaptured Jerusalem and the temple, throwing off the rule of the Greek emperors. They cleansed and rededicated the temple in 164 B.C. A third book, 3 Maccabees, is about the persecution and deliverance of the Jews from under Egyptian rulers at about the same time. It is considered to be deuterocanonical only by a few Orthodox churches. There is also 4 Maccabees, which is a philosophical reflection that uses Jews who died for their faith, recorded in 2 Maccabees, as examples. The book is heavily influenced by Greek philosophy and is not canonical.

The New Testament

While the Old Testament is the Scripture of Israel, the New Testament is the deposit of the faith of the early Christian community. Like many of the books in the Old Testament Apocrypha, the New Testament is written in Greek. The first part of the New Testament includes the four Gospels: Matthew, Mark, Luke, and John. Matthew is the first Gospel in the New Testament, but it is not the earliest one. It is the most obviously Jewish, and probably reflects a time when Christian and non-Christian Jews, especially the Pharisees, were in serious conflict with each other. The best-known part of Matthew is the Sermon on the Mount, which scholars see as a summary of Jesus' ethical teachings. Mark is the shortest Gospel, and probably the earliest. It presents Jesus as a great wonder-worker, with a focus on his passion and death. Luke is the third Gospel, and it builds upon Mark (see Luke 1:1–3). It presents Jesus as the servant of God and savior of the world. The author of Luke continued

New Testament Books

Gospel of Matthew	1–2 Thessalonians
Gospel of Mark	1–2 Timothy
Gospel of Luke	Titus
Gospel of John	Philemon
Acts of the Apostles	Hebrews
Romans	James
1–2 Corinthians	1–2 Peter
Galatians	1–3 John
Ephesians	Jude
Philippians	Revelation
Colossians	

his story with the Acts of the Apostles. The first three Gospels are called the Synoptic Gospels because of their similarity. They see Jesus in much the same way, and "synoptic" means "see together." John is a very different Gospel, and it probably is the latest of the four. It presents the ministry of Jesus in a series of signs and speeches, with profound theological reflection and symbolism.

The second part of the New Testament is referred to as the Epistles because it contains formal letters as well as other writings having addressees. The Acts of the Apostles, written by Luke, continues the story of early Christianity. It tells of the works of the early followers of Jesus, especially Peter and Paul. The emphasis is on the spread of the gospel from Jerusalem to Rome. The letters of Paul, often called the Pauline Epistles, follow the book of Acts. They generally are listed in order of length. Paul's letters were written to churches in various cities across the Roman Empire, and they addressed problems that the believers faced. The epistle to the Romans is the longest and most important of Paul's letters. It was written to the Christians in Rome, before he visited them. It contains the major themes emphasized by the "apostle to the Gentiles," as Paul called himself, in regard to salvation and life in Christ. The two letters sent by Paul to the church in the city of Corinth, 1 and 2 Corinthians, correct a number of serious problems among Christians there. Likewise, Paul's other letters contain the apostle's teachings and advice to the Christians in those areas. The last four letters of Paul are written to individuals, but also to the churches in which those individuals served. These are 1 and 2 Timothy, Titus, and Philemon.

The next part of the New Testament, containing letters not from Paul, often is referred to as the General Epistles. This is because they are written to the Christian community in general, and thus are less specific in their audience. Hebrews is an anonymous letter or sermon written to Jewish Christians. It sets forth the superiority of Jesus Christ over his forerunners in Judaism. James is a kind of Christian wisdom book, probably written by James the brother of Jesus, who was an important leader in the early church. The epistles 1 and 2 Peter are from Peter, the chief of the apostles, although many scholars doubt that 2 Peter came from Peter himself. These epistles encourage Christians during times of persecution. Jude is a short sermon or letter, from Jude the brother of James (and therefore of Jesus), warning Christians against those who would divide and deceive them. The epistles 1, 2, and 3 John are very similar in style and theology to the Gospel of John. They deal with some problems that came up in churches known to the "elder" John.

The final text of the New Testament is the book of Revelation, also known as the Apocalypse. As the name implies, it is a type of apocalyptic book, similar to parts of Daniel and Ezekiel. Revelation focuses on Jesus Christ as the Lord of history, and his battle with evil. It is highly symbolic, and the right way to

understand this book is a matter of much debate an̄
tians. Many Christians believe that the book predict
symbolic way, future events, including the return of Christ.

The New Testament Canon

Unlike their use of varying Old Testament canons, Orthodox, Catholic, and Protestant Christians accept an identical New Testament canon. The books of the New Testament are writings that the early church found valuable and insightful for the Christian life. As the church grew, these writings were copied and reread wherever the gospel spread. From collected texts such as the Muratorian Canon, dated about A.D. 200, we know that the early church actively embraced most books included in the present list. They also excluded several that were being circulated among the churches. For example, the four Gospels and the Acts of the Apostles were accepted, but the Letter to the Laodiceans was rejected as illegitimate. Other books, such as the Shepherd of Hermas (ca. A.D. 90–140), were affirmed for Christian reading, but they could not be used in worship, because they were written too long after Christ's death and resurrection.

From these examples, we can see that a consensus on which books were authoritative began to emerge early in the development of the church. The writings chosen for Christian worship and teaching were selected based on their authenticity, wide acceptance among churches, and close proximity to the time of Jesus' earthly ministry. The first "official" consensus on the contents of the New Testament canon took place at the Council of Laodicea (A.D. 363). This council did not list the book of Revelation. The entire New Testament canon as it now exists is recorded in an important Easter letter from the great bishop of Alexandria, Athanasius (A.D. 367). This same list was also confirmed at the Synod of Carthage (A.D. 397). Since the fourth century, a general consensus has existed about the books of the New Testament canon.

Bible Translations

We have already seen that the Bible was translated very early on into Greek and Latin. Because Scripture is important for the spiritual life of every Christian, the Bible has been translated from the original Hebrew and Greek into many other languages. The Latin Vulgate was the Bible of the West until the Reformation in the sixteenth century. Since then, the most influential English version, or translation, of the Bible has been the Authorized Version, better known as the King James Version (A.D. 1611). The Revised Standard Version, the New Revised Standard Version, the American Standard Version, the New American Standard Version, and the New King James Version all are built upon it. Other popular translations of the Bible in English include the New International Version, the New English Bible, the Good News Bible (Today's English Version), the New American Bible, the New Jerusalem Bible, and the Revised English Bible. In addition to numerous translations, there are also several "paraphrase" editions of Scripture, such as the Living Bible. The difference between a translation and a paraphrase is one of degree. The Bible translator seeks to create a readable and well-crafted translation that remains as faithful to the original language as possible. The creator of a paraphrase works to simplify a translation in order to make it more understandable in a particular cultural context.

In all of its various versions and translations, the Bible is the best selling book in the world. Few would disagree that it is the single most influential book in Western culture, and continues to inspire and challenge Christians and non-Christians alike. As we have seen, the "book of books" contains a number of different types of writings. The works are all quite old, and they include stories about the beginning of humankind and visions of how the world will end. Christians look to this book to understand who Jesus is, to know their past, and to learn how they should live now. Scripture provides believers both with a resource for structuring their life as the church and with answers to the questions that life brings.

Questions for Further Reflection

1. Why are there so many different translations of the Bible in English?

2. What are some of the ways in which the Bible has been influential in Western literature and culture? Why has it had such a significant impact?

3. What stories or parts of the Bible do you find most meaningful for your life, and why? If none, why not?

4. What do Christians mean when they say that the Bible is "the Word of God"?

Chapter 6

Common Christian Roots

The Christian family is amazingly diverse. For Christians, this diversity is itself an expression of the creativity of God and the unique message of Jesus Christ. Sometimes, the many variations among denominations and communions are viewed as a sign of disunity in the church. However, at the center of the Christian faith one finds a number of common themes and practices that testify to a common union in Christ Jesus. In this chapter we examine those elements of faith and practice that give definition to Christ's family, the church.

To help us understand the modern shape of this ancient faith, we will look into the history of the church. We will look to the common elements of the Christian heritage, the shared beliefs and practices derived from a long life together as a community of faith. By considering the early church and its development, we can discover things that all followers of Jesus should share. The history of the early church and its development, centered on the person of Jesus Christ, provides common roots for all believers. This heritage weaves a common pattern through contemporary Christian life, organization, doctrine, creed, and worship.

Our story of Jesus and his followers spans four periods: New Testament, *Patristic, Medieval,* and *Modern.* The New Testament period encompasses most of the first century; it begins with the birth of Jesus and ends after the death of the last apostle. The Patristic period begins a short time after the death of the last apostle and encompasses the years A.D. 100–500. The Medieval period covers approximately ten centuries, A.D. 500–1500. The Modern period extends from A.D. 1500 to the present. Although these dates are approximate, they help us identify major transitions in the development of the church.

Christianity begins during the New Testament period, a time of dramatic social and political upheaval in Jerusalem. During this time, the followers of Jesus Christ witnessed his teaching and miracles, his love and compassion, and his death at the hands of Roman authorities. Three days after Jesus' death, they also witnessed his resurrection from the dead, and then the beginning of the church. The Patristic period is that of the early church. The word "Patristic" refers to "fathers," and it draws upon the idea of Christians as family. Christians call the men and women of the early church the "fathers" and "mothers" of the church because their work developed, extended, and strengthened the Christian community. Because their work nurtured and guided the first centuries of Christianity, the church honors them with these titles. The Medieval period, or Middle Ages, refers to that time between classical or Greco-Roman times and the modern period. Finally, the Modern period simply refers to what is new and up-to-date. This period may well take on a different name in the future, when a postmodern culture, already forming, fully establishes itself.

The New Testament Period

Our overview begins with the New Testament period. Christianity began as a religious movement among Jews, but it soon spread beyond Palestine to Egypt, Syria, and Greece. Jesus was crucified, put to death on a cross, about A.D. 33. His followers, who witnessed his death, also testified to his resurrection from the dead. As word of this spread, believers met together

Patristic Period

A.D.

45–90	The Apostolic age. The New Testament and other early Christian documents are written.
70	The fall of Jerusalem to the Roman army.
152	Justin Martyr writes his *Apology*.
177	Irenaeus becomes bishop of Lyons.
ca. 210	Origen of Alexandria begins his work as teacher and theologian.
270	St. Anthony begins his life as a monk in Egypt.
313	Edict of Milan. Constantine the Great ends persecution of Christians.
325	Council of Nicea. Source of the Nicene Creed.
451	Council of Chalcedon on the two natures of Christ.

for worship. Soon after Jesus' resurrection, a large group of Christians assembled. While they were together, the power of God came over the group, and many there saw flames flicker over their heads, while some also received the ability to speak in foreign languages. These strange events had a powerful effect on Jesus' followers. This time when Christians gathered after the death and resurrection of Christ is the beginning of the church. Believers carried the message of Jesus across the

The Destruction of the Jewish Temple

The destruction of the Jewish temple occurred in A.D. 70. It was destroyed by command of Titus, during the reign of the Roman emperor Vespasian. The temple had become the focal point for Jewish revolt. The temple has never been rebuilt, but parts of its formidable foundation still exist.

Roman Empire, and people from all backgrounds became followers of Jesus Christ. The church grew rapidly, and the ever increasing number of new converts brought many challenges for the leaders of the faith.

By the time of the fall of Jerusalem in A.D. 70, the religion that formed around Jesus Christ had spread through many of the larger cities of the Roman Empire and out to the East. The Roman Empire had conquered and incorporated a number of cultures and people, and the Christian faith soon included many Gentiles. Although the followers of Jesus Christ are taught to love their enemies, do good works, be respectful to authorities, and care for one another, this "new" religion seemed threatening to both Jewish and Roman authorities. At times, this made Christians the target of persecution by both groups. Jewish authorities objected to the Christian claim that Jesus Christ was the long-awaited savior of Israel.

The question of why the Romans persecuted Christians is more complex. The Romans held a large empire together through force, but also through a policy of cultural assimilation and religious tolerance. Roman rulers often allowed those whom they had conquered to continue the worship of popular local gods. However, for reasons of state unity, the Romans insisted that their citizens respect the empire by worshiping the "genius of the emperor." This was accepted by most, largely because the addition of a few Roman gods to an already large set of deities was not a great inconvenience. After all, they thought, the gods of the Roman Empire must be powerful, since Rome had conquered so many great nations. In this light, to worship the emperor and the divine powers that supported him could be a very good thing indeed.

The Romans respected the power of religion and believed that the gods protected the state. Religion existed to serve the state and to bring it prosperity and peace. Refusal to worship the gods could lead to calamity for the nation. All people were required to pay appropriate honor to the gods of Rome, because the health of the empire depended upon it. The only exception was allowed to Jews. This exception was granted out of deference to the ancient and respected religion that they practiced. Special status was granted to Jews because they were strict *monotheists,* people who worship only one god. Instead of worshiping the emperor, they were required to pray for the emperor and the empire. This special status, however, did not extend to Christians, even though they worshiped the same God as did the Jews. Christianity, which the Romans had first treated as a kind of Judaism, soon was identified as a new religion of its own.

The Christian religion was seen as a threat to the empire because believers proclaimed Christ as their "Lord" and met in secret places. Believers refused to worship idols, and they were accused of atheism because they worshiped an "invisible" God. The Christian practices of baptizing and holding a communion meal led to rumors that Christ's followers drowned babies and ate the flesh of dead human beings. Christians also were scorned for their association with the lower classes and for their acceptance of slaves and women as equals before God. Roman authorities, charged with maintaining the empire, saw

The Martyr Polycarp

Polycarp (ca. A.D. 69–155) was an important early martyr for the Christian faith. He was a leader of the church and bishop of Smyrna. The elderly Christian was at least eighty years old when he was arrested by Roman authorities. Because of his refusal to recant his Christian faith, he was burned to death, in a public spectacle.

the early Christians as a threat. To become a Christian was often dangerous, and sometimes even fatal. In some cases, those who refused to worship Roman gods and renounce Christ were tortured or killed for their faith. These people are known as *martyrs,* from a Greek word meaning "witnesses." The stories of their lives and deaths, and even their burial places, were remembered with reverence by the Christian community.

These believers had given up their lives, just as Jesus did, and they were greatly admired. Despite the Romans' effort to suppress the Christian movement, it grew very rapidly. Estimates are difficult, but some scholars think that by A.D. 300, about 10 percent of the Roman Empire was Christian. The new faith was also spreading into Asia and Africa.

The Patristic Period

Why did the early Christian faith spread so rapidly? Again, there are many causes for this growth. The old Roman religions were observed more as custom than devotion, as a form of religion without power. The sincerity, good works, and religious zeal of the Christians must have been attractive. The fact that Christianity had only one God and a clear set of moral teachings might also have had its appeal. Christians accepted all people equally, for all were one in Christ. This openness attracted slaves, women, and the lower classes — groups not treated with equality in Greco-Roman culture. Christians formed a community of love and service, with a sense of higher calling and noble, lofty goals. This sense of belonging and purpose must have been attractive to many other people. Finally, the attractiveness of Jesus and his teachings, once studied, must have been part of the reason for the growth of Christianity.

During this time of growth many difficulties facing the earliest Christians came from nonbelievers, but still others came from inside the fellowship of faith. Early believers were challenged to defend the faith against claims made against it. These early defenders were called *apologists,* and their task was to present a reasoned defense of the Christian faith. Not only did Christianity have to be defended against misunderstandings about worship practices, but also the teachings of Christ had to be explained to the intellectuals of the Roman Empire, many of whom were critical of the new faith. The church also had to guard against division and misunderstanding within the body of Christ itself. Religious rites, sacred texts, and doctrinal teachings had to be set forth clearly. In this way, the followers of Christ could embrace what was true to the faith and relinquish beliefs and practices that were not. This process took many years and required the early church to overcome numerous challenges.

During this early period of persecution and growth (ca. A.D. 100–300), Christianity faced a number of internal difficulties. As we have seen, Jesus was himself a Jew, as were his earliest followers. They understood the coming of Jesus Christ as Messiah because they shared the common Scripture of the

Jewish religion. Their ritual practices were Jewish, and their heritage gave them a common theological foundation. However, the Christian faith spread rapidly, with a growing number of converts spread across the vast Roman Empire. New converts heard the message of Jesus Christ, that God loved them, and that the way of the cross made it possible to be forgiven for sin. However, the Jewish understanding of Hebrew Scripture, and even more basic concepts such as monotheism, were foreign to the Hellenistic cultures of the Greco-Roman world. The church soon grew beyond its Jewish identity, especially after the destruction of Jerusalem by the Romans in A.D. 70.

Growing into Egypt, North Africa, Syria, Persia, Asia Minor, and Greece, the early church had no established list of biblical books, no set liturgy, and no official theology. With no clear identity established, the followers of Christ struggled to learn what it means to be the family of God in the midst of many different cultures. Cultural differences and geographical isolation created a great diversity of belief and practice, which was not always embraced as a positive value by church leaders. The church also had to combat false teachings and incorrect beliefs about God, beliefs that often entered the fellowship when converts from other religions tried to understand and explain Jesus Christ. As the Christian gospel spread and was translated into various cultures and tongues, differences in practice and interpretation were inevitable.

A number of early Christian writings, including many in the New Testament, are letters and advice correcting errors in worship and doctrine that occurred at times in the church. The most important of these writings are known as the *Apostolic Fathers,* a group of early writings from a variety of authors, written in Greek, during the late first and early second centuries. During this early period the Christians applied and extended their devotion to Jesus Christ. They continued to worship him, tell stories about his life and teachings, and spread the good news.

As the good news of Jesus Christ gained acceptance, the work of the apologists gained new importance. One of the most important of these was Justin Martyr (ca. A.D. 100–165), a Roman philosopher who converted to Christianity. He wrote several works, two of which were called an "apology," or intellectual defense of the faith. He defended Christianity against pagan and Jewish intellectuals. Another person who helped pagans understand Christian teachings was the famous scholar Clement of Alexandria (ca. A.D. 155–220). Clement battled non-Christian teachings such as Gnosticism. This was a philosophy found in some Jewish, Christian, and pagan sects. It was a combination of many popular Greek and Asian ideas, with a focus on salvation by way of secret knowledge (*gnosis*, in Greek) revealed through enlightened teachers. It was also dualistic in its view of the universe. Found in many Greco-Roman and Asian religions and philosophies, dualism divides reality into two parts: light and dark, spiritual and material, good and evil. For the Gnostics, salvation by secret knowledge meant an escape from the physical world. The Christian form of Gnosticism was popular in Egypt, Asia Minor, and Greece. Gnostics formed their own small groups in churches, and they had secret documents, such as the Gospel of Thomas. Other great Christian teachers and writers, such as Irenaeus (ca. A.D. 125–94) in Gaul (now France) and Tertullian (ca. A.D. 160–215) in North Africa, wrote long books in opposition to the Gnostics and their teachings.

As the church explained itself and its message, it began to encounter problems of **heresy**. A heresy is an idea rejected by the church as a distortion or misunderstanding of the Christian faith. To protect the faith from internal and external opposition, the church developed the institutions of creed, bishop, and canon. A creed is a formulation that sets forth the standard beliefs of a religious group. The word "creed" comes from the Latin word for "believe." The importance of creeds for the

> ### Gnostic Scripture
>
> One early Christian heretic, Marcion, created his own Bible, with only one Gospel and a few Epistles of Paul. The Gnostics, too, had their own Epistles, Gospels, and Acts.

early church is seen in a very early document known as the *Apostles' Creed.* This text was used in various forms in Christian worship. During baptism, new Christians were asked to clearly state their beliefs about the Father, the Son, and the Holy Spirit. The reply to these questions became standardized, and this formula became known much later as the Apostles' Creed. The earliest official creed is the *Nicene Creed* of A.D. 325. Written to combat Arianism, a heresy that taught that Jesus was divine but of a different nature than God, the Nicene Creed affirmed the idea that Jesus was both fully human and fully divine. The *Council of Chalcedon,* in A.D. 451, continued to expand and defend the Nicene doctrine of Christ.

The writings known as the Apostolic Fathers give us a window into the practices and beliefs of the early church. Following the death of the apostles, and given the problems facing the church, it is no wonder that leadership became crucial. Bishops gained in power and prestige, and they became important teachers. The bishop was the Christian leader of a city and its surrounding regions. Under the bishop, the pastor or priest presided over the local church meetings. At the next level, *deacons* helped the church with its financial and missionary work. During this early period, and on up to the time of Constantine the Great, church leadership was open to women and men, and to slaves and free citizens alike. However, the role of the bishop took on more of a Roman flavor over time. Slaves

The Apostles' Creed
(late second century)

- I believe in God, the Father Almighty, creator of heaven and earth.

- I believe in Jesus Christ, his only son, our Lord. He was conceived by the power of the Holy Spirit and born to the Virgin Mary. He suffered under Pontius Pilate, was crucified, died, and was buried. He descended to the dead. On the third day, he rose again. He ascended into heaven and is seated at the right hand of the Father. He will come again to judge the living and the dead.

- I believe in the Holy Spirit, the holy catholic church, the communion of saints, the forgiveness of sins, the resurrection of the body, and the life everlasting.

The name "Apostles' Creed" is based upon an old legend that the twelve apostles each contributed a portion of the text. Although not technically a creed, it does provide us with the earliest summary of Christian beliefs outside the New Testament.

and women were excluded from leadership after Christianity became an official religion in the fourth century.

Women disciples played an important part in the early Christian church. From the earliest times, women were attracted to the Jesus movement and became disciples. Mary Magdalene,

The Christogram

The sign under which Constantine conquered is traditionally believed to be what is now called the Christogram, or Chi-Rho. This early symbol for Christ was formed by superimposing the Greek letters *X* (chi) and *P* (rho) on top of one another. They are the first two letters in the Greek word for "Christ."

Priscilla the companion of Paul, the apostle Junia, and the deacon Phoebe are examples of women leaders and the important roles that they played in the early church. In fact, in the New Testament, whenever the leadership of a house church is mentioned by name, it is either a woman, or a woman and a man. We have evidence from Christian burial places of women who were priests and bishops before the age of Constantine. But the role of women in the early church decreased as the church became more institutionalized and "respectable."

Greek and Roman leadership was male oriented. As the Christian movement became more Roman, women gradually were excluded from official leadership in the church. The same story, for the most part, is true also of slaves and the poor. Slavery and poverty were common in the Greco-Roman world. Jesus' message of equality for all people was attractive to the lower classes. Many of the early Gentile Christian converts probably were slaves, and all of the twelve apostles came from humble origins. But as the church grew in scope and power, its leadership became better educated, and was drawn from free and noble families. This growth toward Roman acceptability reached its height under Constantine.

Constantine the Great was the first emperor to become a Christian. Just before an important battle, Constantine had a dream in which Christ showed him the cross and told him, "In this sign, conquer." Constantine was a great general, and he unified the entire Roman Empire under his control. He stopped the persecution of Christians with the Edict of Milan in A.D. 313. Constantine favored Christians in his political and social policies. This made Christianity even more popular, and the church grew in influence and power.

Constantine also sought to unify the church in its theology. It was he who called the Council of Nicea in A.D. 325 to establish the correct teachings of the church about God and Christ. Christian leaders who refused to accept the teachings of Nicea were excommunicated — that is, forced to leave the church. The emperor added his political weight, and sometimes they also were exiled from the empire. This unification of church and state was a major influence on the development of Christianity over the centuries, especially in Europe.

The Middle Ages

Constantine moved the capital of the empire from Rome to Constantinople (modern Istanbul, Turkey). The political power of the empire gradually shifted from West to East. When the city of Rome fell to invading tribes of Goths, Vandals, and Huns, a power vacuum was left behind. The Roman Empire that remained, in the East, is called the Byzantine Empire by modern historians. As leaders and government officials fled or were killed, the church and the pope (the bishop of Rome) were forced to use their power and organization to maintain civilization and stability in the West. In this atmosphere, the power of the pope grew, and he began to take on political as well as religious influence.

The first pope to openly proclaim himself as the head of the entire church was Leo I, who reigned from A.D. 440 to 461. He saved the city of Rome from Attila the Hun in A.D. 452, and increased the prestige and power of the pope throughout Western Europe and North Africa. The authority of the *papacy,* the office of the pope, increased even more under the wise rule of Gregory the Great (A.D. 540–604).

The theology of the church was also unified in the period from Constantine the Great to Gregory the Great (A.D. 300–600). A series of council and synods debated the true nature of God. The doctrine of the Trinity — the understanding that the one true God exists as Father, Son, and Holy Spirit — was developed and defended. Christian orthodoxy — meaning correct or standard thinking — also developed a more thorough Christology. Jesus was declared at the Council of Chalcedon (A.D. 451) to be both fully God and fully human, without any mixing of the two. The canon of the Bible also was settled.

Included in this organizational growth and stability was Christian worship. After Christianity became the official religion of the Roman Empire in A.D. 392, many more churches established buildings in which to worship. Worship and liturgy became more standardized, and an organized *clergy* of ordained church leaders gained more prominence. Especially important to this growing stability were the power and influence of the bishops, who were understood to be the leading teachers and spokespersons for Christianity for the cities in which they lived.

During the times of persecution before Constantine, many Christians died for their faith. These martyrs were much admired by the Christian church for the strength of their belief. Sometimes the early Christians celebrated communion meals in

---

The Seven Ecumenical Councils
of the Church

A series of seven councils, held during the period from A.D. 325 to 787, are known as the ecumenical councils. They are called "ecumenical" because they represent the theological beliefs of the universal church. The councils were held in the period before divisions led to church schism in 1054. The seven ecumenical councils are:

Council of Nicea (A.D. 325)

Council of Constantinople (A.D. 381)

Council of Ephesus (A.D. 431)

Council of Chalcedon (A.D. 451)

Council of Constantinople (A.D. 553)

Council of Constantinople II (A.D. 680–81)

Council of Nicea (A.D. 787)

---

the catacombs (underground tombs) just to be near the bodies of these dead saints. Miracles were attributed to the holy relics, or remains, of the martyrs. This was the beginning of a common practice among Catholics and Orthodox that continues today: saints and martyrs are remembered and venerated (respected and revered, but not worshiped) for their Christian witness and life.

Icons, which are pictorial images of the saints or special events in the life of the church, were especially beloved. As part of this veneration, believers asked dead saints and martyrs to intercede for them. These saints and martyrs, wise and courageous Christians in their lives on earth, were understood to be alive after death and present in heaven with Christ. Their presence in heaven placed them closer to God, so their prayers may be better heard than those of the humble Christian on earth. Over time, and especially during the Middle Ages, the Virgin Mary (the mother of Jesus) became the chief of the saints. Also, patron saints began to be associated with certain causes, occupations, groups, or nations. Although these practices are not directly encouraged by the church and are rejected by Protestants, they continue to be popular among many Christians.

Martyrdom was never something that Christians were encouraged to seek. However, those who felt that they were spiritually strong enough to face death in the name of Christ were honored and revered. Along with martyrdom, the life of prayer and spiritual discipline was very important to the early Christians. The practices associated with the disciplined spiritual life were explored and refined in the period after the legalization of Christianity. Under Constantine the Great, the persecution of the early church came to an end, and as the church grew in importance, power, wealth, and acceptance, it adopted many of the social and court practices of the Roman Empire. Many Christians rejected this "imperialism" in the faith and moved into secluded areas, such as deserts and forests, in response. There, in their solitude, they prayed and fasted on behalf of the church, which they believed was becoming too worldly.

With the end of persecution and martyrdom, some Christians believed that the highest calling of a Christian was to surrender worldly pleasures in order to live a life of holy poverty and prayer. These devoted Christians were called monks (men) and nuns (women), and their way of life is called monastic. The words "monk" and "monastic" come from the Greek word for "single, alone," and the word "nun" derives from a Latin title of respect for an older woman. These Christians gave up marriage and sex, family and feasting, to live solitary lives of prayer.

The most famous early monk was St. Anthony (ca. A.D. 251–356), who lived alone in the Egyptian desert. Pachomius, who lived about the same time and also was from Egypt, believed that monks should often be alone, but also live and work next to each other for worship and support. He founded one of the first *monasteries,* and his sister Mary founded one of the first *convents.* Pachomius also created rules for their community life. In Western Europe, the most famous and influential rules for monks were written by Benedict of Nursia (ca. A.D. 480–550). His *Rule* was so wise and reasonable that many copied it, and it became the standard for the monastic movement. His religious *order,* or movement, is called Benedictine, and it still has tens of thousands of members today.

Entering monastic life was a way to say no to the values of the world. Monks and nuns lived lives of silence and virtual solitude in monasteries. Some, of course, became literal solitaries as hermits. In both cases, such people prayed and fasted on behalf of a church that they believed was becoming too worldly. From the ranks of such monks frequently came the great reforming popes and bishops of the Eastern and Western branches of the church. Some monasteries themselves became immensely wealthy, despite being founded as retreats from worldly wealth.

Helped in part by the leadership of monks and the stability of large monasteries, the church grew and spread throughout the early part of the Middle Ages. However, a schism between the Latin-speaking Catholics and the Greek-speaking Orthodox was looming on the horizon. With the fall of Rome in the fifth century, the Roman Empire was cut in two. Social and cultural development followed different paths in East and West, and a variety of conflicts and disagreements contributed to tension between them. One area of tension was *evangelism.* For example, the Orthodox sent missionaries to the Slavs in Eastern Europe, an area also of interest to the Catholics. The famous missionaries and monks Cyril and Methodius were opposed by Latin-speaking missionaries to the same area. Eventually, the kingdom of Russia became Orthodox rather than Catholic, and it is interesting to note that the king of Russia thought that these were two different religions. Another point of conflict was religious authority. Rome had long claimed supremacy in church leadership, based upon apostolic succession in the line of the apostle Peter. Catholics argued that the pope, as the bishop of Rome, is the chief minister of Christ and the head of the church on earth. By contrast, the Orthodox Church held that the model for leadership was that of several equal and autonomous bishops with their own claims to legitimate apostolic succession. These issues contributed to the first major split in the Christian family. In an event known as the Great Schism, the Orthodox and Catholic traditions split in A.D. 1054.

Part of the context for the Great Schism was the rise of *Islam* as a world power. In A.D. 622, the prophet Muhammad was opposed by the people of Mecca in Arabia. He took refuge in Medina, a small oasis not far away. This was the beginning of Islam, and Muslims date their calendar from this year. Islam is a post-Christian religion that draws upon Jewish and Christian sources. By the time Muhammad died, in A.D. 632, a large part of the Arabian populace already had left their idols behind for Islam. The armies of the caliphs, who were Muslim political leaders, swept over the sands of the Middle East and North Africa, where Islam is still the dominant religion. They spread all the way into Spain from North Africa, and were finally stopped at the Battle of Tours (A.D. 732) by Charles Martel, also known as Charles the Hammer. In the East, Islam ran into the Byzantine Empire, which also halted its expansion into Europe. The armies of the caliphs also expanded eastward as far as India.

Just as Muslim empires were settling down after tremendous expansion, the West found a new leader in the son of

Medieval Period

530	St. Benedict begins his order and his *Rule* is written.
590	Gregory the Great becomes pope.
ca. 650	Christian missionaries reach China.
800	Charlemagne crowned emperor.
863	Cyril and Methodius bring Christianity to the Slavs.
988	Russia becomes Christian (Orthodox).
1054	Great Schism: Orthodox East and Catholic West split.
1095	Pope Urban II launches the Crusades.
1200	University of Paris founded; scholastic theology begins.
1202	Fourth Crusade; Crusaders attack Constantinople.
1206	Francis of Assisi begins his ministry, founds his order.
ca. 1380	John Wycliffe leaves Oxford; English Bible translation begun.
1415	John Hus burned as a heretic.
1453	Constantinople (Byzantium) falls to Muslim Turks.
1454	Gutenburg Bible is printed.
1478	Catholic Reformation begins in Spain.

Charles Martel, called Charles the Great, or Charlemagne. He was crowned by the pope on Christmas Day, A.D. 800, to be the new Holy Roman Emperor. Charlemagne was in fact a German, and his empire was in what we now call France. It was neither holy, nor Roman, nor an empire. However, the dream of Roman power lingered in the minds of Western people during those hard times. Because of the backward and difficult conditions of those times, we now call them the Dark Ages. Few, if any, cultural or religious advances came out of Europe. Byzantium and the Arabic empires were far more advanced. But Charlemagne represented the beginnings of a new stability and a slow return to power and importance in Western Europe after the fall of Rome and the rise of Islam.

With the growth of a new empire, and the pope as spiritual leader of the West, Europe was able to battle the Muslim powers in the Middle East. For the glory of God and Christ, for the hope of heaven and for earthly power and influence, European soldiers and knights went on the Crusades. The first Crusade was launched by Pope Urban II in A.D. 1095, during the Council of Clermont. The hope was for a great Western army that would go forth, for the glory of God and the Catholic Church, to save Constantinople from the Muslims. In this way they would rescue the "Holy Land" of Palestine and the "Holy City" of Jerusalem. In the beginning, the Crusaders did accomplish some of their goals. However, in the long run, the cost in terms of suffering, life, and funds was hardly worth it. The Holy Land was in the hands of Crusaders for about a century, and then it returned to Islam through the power of a united Muslim army. Soldiers in the Fourth Crusade, aware of the wealth in the Christian city of Constantinople, attacked and decimated the city. Thus, the Crusades helped to bring and end to the Christian empire of Byzantium, which they were called to protect. Constantinople fell to the Turks in A.D. 1453. The Orthodox

Christians and the Muslim cultures of the world have never forgotten or forgiven this aggression on the part of Western Europe.

The Crusades did demonstrate the growing power and wealth of Western Europe and the Catholic Church. They also were one manifestation of the political power of the pope in Europe. As the church grew in power and wealth, corruption followed. Religious orders of monks and nuns, founded to minister in the name of the church, proved to be a source of religious reform. The most famous of these was Francis of Assisi, whose life of poverty and simplicity contrasted markedly with the wealth of the Catholic leadership. This "troubadour for Christ" founded the Franciscan Order, and his friend and fellow saint, Clare of Assisi, founded the Order of Poor Clares in the thirteenth century.

From the thirteenth century onward, Europe began to grow in power, wealth, and learning based in large part on ideas and riches brought back from the East during the Crusades. One manifestation of this was the growing power of towns, and of craftsmen and tradesmen in those towns. Another sign of growing cultural stability was the appetite for higher education and the founding of Christian universities in Bologna, Paris, and Oxford. As people became better educated, the romance of the Roman Empire attracted their imaginations and drew their minds back to Greco-Roman literature. This concern for the sources of Western culture was known as the **Renaissance,** or "rebirth" of classical culture, which began in Italy during the fourteenth century. The Renaissance represented the flowering of Western Medieval culture, and also its end. As the flow of ideas increased, the authoritarianism and corruption of the church became unacceptable. Prominent Catholic Renaissance scholars, such as John Wycliffe (died A.D. 1384) in Oxford and John Hus (put to death in A.D. 1415) in Prague, added their voices to the call for reform of the church.

Toward the Modern Period

The end of the Middle Ages saw the end of a unified **Christendom,** a period of unity of church and state in the West. Although church reform did see some success, Catholics who called for radical reforms were excommunicated and condemned by the leadership in Rome. However, based upon Renaissance learning and new freedom to travel and spread ideas and technologies, the reformers would stage a successful revolt against Catholic power and corruption. This was known as the Protestant movement, and it began with a former monk in Germany named Martin Luther. We will take up this story in the next chapter.

To review: The first fourteen centuries of Christianity provided important common themes that defined and shaped a new religious movement. The canon of the New Testament was agreed upon, and the Bible was translated into many languages. The basic beliefs of the Christian faith were hammered out in councils and written down in creeds. The order of church political life developed and was stabilized through a network of bishops and priests, as well as written and unwritten regulations. The form of worship in the Christian religion, despite much regional variation, was given an overall shape and structure. Christianity, in short, became a world religion. But along with power, stability, and order came the corruption, arrogance, greed, and hatred that would rend the body of Christ and bring dishonor to the name "Christian." Despite these setbacks, the growth of Christianity brought much that was beneficial to the world. The message of the poor carpenter from Galilee, and the devoted love and service of his followers, inspired millions with a vision of peace, loving service, and a common life together in unity. Although the church itself never quite lived up to this vision, it was an indispensable torchbearer, passing on the light of Christ from generation to generation.

Questions for Further Reflection

1. What positive role did heresy play in the development of the church?

2. What changes, positive and negative, did the reign of Constantine the Great bring to the church?

3. What role did the ecumenical councils play in the development of the church?

4. What changes did the Middle Ages bring to Christianity?

5. Even though Christians are so diverse, are there ways in which it is apparent that all come from common Christian roots?

Chapter 7

Denominations and Difference

We have noted in earlier chapters that the church is a diverse body of believers drawn from many different cultures and communities. This is seen in the diversity of Christian worship styles and in the many ways Christians express their devotion and obedience to God. As followers of Jesus Christ, they believe that this diversity is a gift from God. The New Testament teaches that God gives everyone different talents and gifts, and intends for these to be shared with others. In this way, we recognize our need for one another, and we learn to value and respect those who are different from us. At the center of Christian diversity stands Jesus Christ, their one common Lord. Their common love for God and their obedience to the teachings of Jesus Christ create unity within diversity. All followers of Christ belong to one spiritual family. This Christian family is called the church, and it has many branches, each one reflecting a unique tradition or history.

Each one of the many traditions within the church reveals something unique about the story of God and his people. Together, these distinctive traditions are part of a larger Christian history, a heritage of wisdom and experience passed down from previous generations of Christians. Tradition bears witness to God's faithfulness in the lives of those preceding generations of believers. It is a testimony to the fact that through Christ, believers are bound together in a community that transcends the bounds of time and space. This is important for Christians, since they believe that the life they begin in Jesus Christ will never end. Christians look forward to an eternity in the presence of God and in the company of the saints. It is fitting, then, that the wisdom that comes in Christian tradition is honored and respected.

In chapter 6 we traced the growth of Christian tradition from the early church period to the dawn of the Modern period. Our story began with the growth of Christianity from a small, persecuted religious movement into the official religion of the Roman Empire. From there, we noted that Christianity flourished undivided until A.D. 1054, when the church split between East (Orthodox) and West (Catholic). Though many reasons are given for the separation of Eastern and Western Christianity, the church East and West continued to grow in ways that reflected cultural differences, and these changes are still evident today. Six centuries later, the Western church underwent another division, when the Protestant movement began. In this chapter we will examine the origin of the most prominent branches, or denominations, that originated in the Protestant movement.

The Protestants

The growth of the Christian denominations we see about us today in the West can be traced back to the sixteenth century and the Protestant Reformation. This was a period when many leaders and teachers in the Western church sought to reform the church of God. As scholars, they learned Hebrew and Greek in order to study the Bible in its original languages. Here we see the influence of Renaissance learning upon the Protestant movement. The Renaissance period brought with it a renewed interest in antiquities and the study of ancient texts in the original languages. It also emphasized the importance of education for the common people. All of the early Protestant leaders were Renaissance scholars.

Martin Luther (1484–1546), like John Wycliffe and Jan Hus before him, wanted to reform the church on the basis of the Bible. This focus upon Scripture as the most authoritative source of guidance for Christian faith and practice is reflected in the work of the Reformation. The "cry of the Reformation" has been summarized in three Latin slogans: *sola scriptura, sola fides,* and *sola gratia.* The ideas that these slogans capture are simple yet important for the history of Christian belief and practice. *Sola scriptura* is the principle that the church must base its doctrines, practices, and ethics on the Bible alone. *Sola fides* teaches that salvation from sin does not come from living a good life or doing good deeds, but from putting one's faith in Jesus Christ. Salvation is a free gift of God and cannot be earned; it comes *sola gratia*, through grace alone.

This theological revolution went alongside a major social and political revolution. With its emphasis upon Scripture and on the responsibilities and authority of individual believers, Reformation theology challenged many ideas and prerogatives of the Catholic Church. Common practices such as the veneration of the saints were questioned, as was the power of the pope. Luther believed that Scripture pointed to Christ as the only true head of the church. Luther's teachings also caused many to reconsider their call to the monastic life. He taught that any job a Christian does, when pleasing to God, is a calling, or vocation, from the Lord. All labor that is pleasing to God and done according to God's purpose is an appropriate expression of religious devotion. To put it another way: God is honored as much by the work of the farmer or the carpenter as by the monk engaged in prayer and spiritual discipline. Because of Luther's teachings, many monks and nuns left religious orders. It is said, without too much exaggeration, that Luther emptied the monasteries of Germany.

Based upon his new theology, Luther left the monastery and criticized the practices of the Catholic Church. He was excommunicated, and he stood in danger of being put to death for his teachings. But times had changed. For one thing, Luther's ideas were spreading rapidly due to the invention of the printing press. For another, the nations of Europe (such as Saxony, where Luther lived) were beginning to feel a certain nationalism and loyalty to their own local language and ruler. The idea that a distant Italian pope should have so much sway over their lives was becoming quite unpopular. For these reasons, Protestant reformers often were protected by their local political rulers. In essence, they were protecting their own political power by protecting the reformers against the power of the Catholic Church. Protestants could move to towns that were more favorable to their movement for protection from Catholic powers. Eventually, terrible wars were waged over independence from the Holy Roman Emperor and the Catholic Church. These are usually called the "Wars of Religion," which took place in France, Germany, Switzerland, and England in the sixteenth and seventeenth centuries. Because political rulers such as kings and princes still believed that the unity of church and state was a necessary foundation for national security, both sides waged war in an effort to regain total religious and political power. The struggle brought terrible suffering to many innocent people. It also created the conditions for the rise of the Enlightenment and the development of modern Europe.

The Reformation on the European Continent

Lutherans — Christians who embraced the reforming ideas of Martin Luther — were the first Protestants. Because the term "Protestant" ("protester") has a negative connotation, they also called themselves Evangelical (from the Greek word for "gospel"). Lutheran Christianity eventually spread over much of Germany and also into the Scandinavian countries. The Lutheran churches of Germany and Sweden, for example, became state churches. Because Martin Luther spent much of his life in the Catholic tradition, Lutherans kept all Catholic worship practices that seemed to them in keeping with Scripture. Lutherans, therefore, still have bishops, and their worship is a simplified form of Catholic liturgy.

In their worship, Lutherans accepted only two of the seven Catholic sacraments: baptism and Holy Communion. They argued that since these are the only two sacraments explicitly commanded by Jesus in the Gospels, they are the only ones that should be observed. Luther rejected the authority of the pope, and believed in the priesthood of all baptized believers. This is reflected in the fact that Protestant ministers are called pastors, not priests.

Ulrich Zwingli (1484–1531) was another early Protestant, whose ideas for reformation developed about the same time as Luther's. Zwingli brought the Reformation to the important Swiss town of Zurich. His work as a reformer was cut short when he was killed defending Zurich against an attack by a neighboring Swiss canton. However, his influence on the Reformation remains significant, particularly because of its impact upon his followers.

Better known and more influential than Zwingli was his younger contemporary John Calvin (1509–64). Calvin was the leader of the Reformation in Geneva, another important city in Switzerland. These two men carried Protestantism one step farther than the Lutherans. Like Luther, they insisted that all Christian practice must be based upon Scripture. They argued that what is not found in Scripture must not be practiced in a church. The Christians who embraced Calvin's reforms are part of the **Reformed** tradition. Worship in these churches is organized around the Bible lesson and the sermon. Because making images of God is prohibited by Scripture (Exodus 20:4), the first **Calvinist** Christians understood this prohibition to include almost all church decoration. In their zeal, they tore down the statues in old church buildings and even destroyed the stained-glass windows and the paintings that decorated the walls. Even today, Reformed churches often are quite plain. Some conservative Calvinist churches still do not allow musical instruments or choirs, preferring to chant psalms from the Bible as their music.

The early followers of Calvin also are famous for insisting that biblical religion must be the basis for government. Geneva, the city where Calvin became an important religious leader, is an important example of this idea. When Calvin first arrived in Geneva, it had a reputation as one of the most immoral cities in Switzerland. All of this eventually changed under Calvin and his political allies. Strict rules concerning public behavior and morality were introduced by the reformers. Despite some initial riots and disturbances, Geneva became a place where the law was respected, children were educated, and widows and the elderly received care.

The movement begun by Zwingli and Calvin was carried from Switzerland into Germany, France, Holland, England, Scotland, and eventually the United States. Calvinists went by many names. In France they were called **Huguenots,** in Scotland they were known as Reformed and Presbyterian, and in England they were the **Puritans.** Regardless of where Calvinist ideas spread, they carried with them an emphasis upon the responsibilities of individual believers and a concern for education. These attitudes, combined with a disciplined life, personal piety, and strict morality, led to prosperity for many Calvinists. This understanding life became known as the "Protestant work ethic," and it contributed to the success of the early Calvinist settlements in America. The success of Calvin's teachings assisted the spread of capitalist and democratic ideas. Calvin and Zwingli were highly educated men, and because of their influence, churches in the Reformed tradition always have valued education. They insist that their pastors be well educated, and they have founded thousands of colleges and universities. For example, Harvard, the oldest college (now a university) in the United States, was founded by Puritans.

The Radical Reformers

In many ways, the Reformed tradition is quite far removed from traditional Catholic practice. Yet there is another group of reform-minded Christians whose changes in church practice went even beyond those considered by the Lutherans or the Calvinists. These "radical reformers" held ideas that are quite commonplace today but were shocking in their day. The most prominent of these groups were the *Anabaptists,* a name meaning "rebaptizers." These radical reformers sought to separate themselves from the secular world to practice only those things found explicitly in Scripture. Often called by the name "Brethren," they insisted that baptism should be only for adults because the Bible gives no examples of infant baptism. According to the Brethren, church membership should be open only to those who have made a profession of faith for themselves. Anabaptists also taught that the church and state should be completely separate from one another, which was a quite radical idea for that time. Because of their beliefs, they were accused of being heretics and revolutionaries, and they were prohibited throughout Europe. They had the unhappy distinction of being a group persecuted by both Catholics and Protestants, and many of them died for their faith. The most influential Anabaptist theologian was Menno Simons (1496–1561). During a time when some Anabaptists were taking up arms against their persecutors, Simons insisted on a literal reading of the Sermon on the Mount (Matthew 5–7). He taught that pacifism, or non-violence, was the true way of Christ. Today the Brethren, the Amish, and the *Mennonites* keep the Anabaptist tradition alive. The Anabaptists also influenced the early Baptist movement in England.

Christianity in England and America

The Reformation in England began for political, as well as theological, reasons. When the pope refused to grant King Henry VIII an annulment of his marriage, simmering theological and political disputes boiled over. In 1534, Henry rejected the authority of the pope, broke with the Catholic tradition, and declared himself to be the supreme head of the church in England. The *Church of England,* also called the Anglican Church, was born. Worship in the Church of England at first resembled that of the Catholic Church. Moderates, such as the reformer Thomas Cranmer (1448–1556), created an English church not too far removed from the Catholic tradition. However, bloody conflicts eventually broke out between those who wished to return to Roman communion, such as Henry's daughter Queen Mary (1516–58), and those who wished to remain independent, such as his daughter Queen Elizabeth I (1533–1603). Under Elizabeth, a compromise was reached that brought standardized liturgy and practice to the English church. What helped organize the Church of England was the *Book of Common Prayer,* written in 1548 by Thomas Cranmer. The book is still considered a masterpiece by many students of liturgy. Also important for Anglican unity was a statement of faith, known as the Thirty-nine Articles (1563), which set forth the central beliefs of the Anglican tradition. Equally important for the English Reformation was the approved translation of a common English Bible. This famous translation is known as the Authorized Version (1611). It is more commonly called the King James Bible, because King James I commissioned it. Since the Reformation, the Anglican tradition has remained associated with English language and culture.

Two prominent groups broke away from the Anglicans and carried English reforms even further. These separatist movements were the Congregationalists and the Baptists. Both were influenced to a certain degree by Anabaptists from Holland. As persecuted movements, all these groups worked underground, and the exact nature of Anabaptist influence is difficult for historians to trace. The Congregationalist tradition held that the local church should be independent of any bishop or government. Like Anabaptists, they saw the church as a fellowship of committed disciples. Their theology was primarily Calvinist in the early period. They were persecuted, and so they sought religious freedom, first in Holland and then in America. The most famous of these "Pilgrims" landed at Plymouth Rock in 1620.

Baptists were destined to grow into a far larger group than their fellow separatists. The Baptist tradition begins in 1612, when English exiles from Holland returned to Britain to form the first Baptist church. They took up the notions of biblical literalism, adult baptism, and a believers' church from the Anabaptist tradition. Like Anabaptists, Baptists insisted upon the separation of church and state. And like other separatists in England, Baptists were officially persecuted for their radical beliefs until the Act of Toleration (1689). Baptist congregations are independent, but usually align themselves into larger bodies in support of joint efforts such as education, *missions,* and relief work. However, they have no bishops or official creeds. Their denominations, such as British Baptists or Southern Baptists, are free associations of independent local churches. Baptist tradition also emphasizes the authority of Scripture and places

Some Key Events
in Modern Church History

1517	Martin Luther begins the Reformation.
1523	Ulrich Zwingli leads the reformation of Zurich.
1525	Anabaptists baptize each other.
1534	Henry VIII declares his Act of Supremacy.
1545	Council of Trent opens.
1548	Thomas Cranmer writes the *Book of Common Prayer.*
1563	Council of Trent concludes.
1612	First Baptist church in England formed.
1620	Pilgrims land in America.
1648	George Fox founds the Quakers (Society of Friends).
1738	Wesley begins his evangelistic ministry.
1816	Richard Allen elected the first bishop of the African Methodist Episcopal Church.
1869–70	First Vatican Council meets.
1906	Azusa Street revival begins the Pentecostal movement.
1910	International Missionary Council begins ecumenical movement.
1948	World Council of Churches founded.
1962–65	Second Vatican Council meets.

great importance on evangelism and missions. This has helped them to become one of the world's largest Protestant groups. Many of the current nondenominational churches are in debt to the Baptist tradition of free and independent congregations.

Another separatist tradition with roots in the English Reformation is the *Society of Friends,* commonly known as the *Quakers* (a name originally applied to them by detractors). These radical separatists were led by George Fox (1624–91), Margaret Fell (1614–1702), and a number of other like-minded *lay* preachers. The Friends movement emphasized the inner light of Christ, the revelation of God in every human conscience. Friends rejected all clergy and liturgy, and they called their buildings "meetinghouses" rather than "churches." They argued for the equality of all men and women, opposed slavery very early on, and were pacifists like the Anabaptists. In keeping with Scripture, Quakers also refused to swear oaths (Matthew 5:33–37). Because Quakers rejected the authority of the Church of England, they were among the most fiercely persecuted of the independent religious movements in England. Though their numbers were never very large by denominational standards, they carried their message around the world and successfully transported their ideas to the New World. The most famous American Quaker was William Penn (1644–1718), a friend of George Fox and founder of the State of Pennsylvania. Because of their beliefs, Quakers earned a well-deserved reputation for honesty and fair dealings with others.

The eighteenth century saw further developments within Protestantism. One of the most important of these was the Methodist movement. Methodism began as an evangelistic movement in England and soon spread around the world. The Methodist tradition traces its roots back to England's greatest evangelist, the Anglican minister John Wesley (1703–91). Along with his friend George Whitefield (1714–70), his brother Charles Wesley (1707–88), and a host of lay preachers, John Wesley worked to bring the good news of Christian faith to everyone. Because of the large numbers of people bypassed by the traditional ministry of the church in England, Methodists had a powerful ministry. They were especially effective among the poor, the sick, and the imprisoned. This approach is central to the *Wesleyan* tradition, which emphasized the need for conversion but also placed a great importance upon living a holy life. For Wesley, this included careful study of the Bible, as well as showing Christ's kindness to those in need. Methodist meetinghouses soon were established in all the major cities of England, and then spread to Scotland, Wales, and the United States. The Methodist movement experienced tremendous growth in the United States during the nineteenth century, primarily as a response to the Second Great Awakening, a period of intense religious fervor and revival. The Methodist tradition today includes the Wesleyan and Holiness denominations, as well as the African Methodist Episcopal Church and the African Methodist Episcopal Church, Zion. These offshoots emerged in the United States during the 1800s, largely in response to issues associated with slavery and racism.

The United States, with its guarantee of religious freedom and its wide diversity of religious practices, has been fertile ground for Christianity. The Protestant Reformation and renewed Catholic missionary activity coincided with the founding of the colonies that would become the United States and with the expansion of European colonies throughout the world. In the United States, the right of religious freedom and the separation of church and state were assured when the American colonies formed their own government. Although religious tolerance is now a widely accepted principle, the absence of a state church was a new idea among governments in the late eighteenth century, when the United States was formed. Because of religious freedom, multiple sects and religious groups grew and prospered in the United States. Some independent and separatist Protestant groups received government charters and founded their own colonies along the eastern coast of America. Roman Catholicism was well represented in the Americas from the sixteenth century, where it was carried into the New World territories and settlements of European countries such as France and Spain. Unfortunately, the missionary efforts usually were accompanied by bloody military oppression of the local natives. The monarchs and soldiers of Spain and Portugal were hungry for gold and power, and the missionaries from Europe worked right beside these violent conquistadors.

The Catholic Reformation

The Catholic tradition has had many reform movements throughout its long history. Each succeeding movement brought renewal to the Catholic Church and helps account for its enduring strength and vitality. During the period that saw the growth of many Protestant groups, Roman Catholics were undergoing their own Reformation within the Catholic tradition. This period is sometimes called the *Counter-Reformation* because it was in many ways a response to the Protestant Reformation. It is probably best to refer to this entire movement, however, as the Catholic Reformation, especially since it began before Luther was born.

The Catholic Reformation was as much an answer to its own internal concerns as it was a response to outside protest. One of the most important events in the Catholic Reformation was the Council of Trent (1545–63). Trent brought accountability and greater organization throughout the Catholic Church. Stronger authority was given to the pope, to bishops, and to priests. Theology and church practice were regulated, and the Mass was affirmed as the center of Catholic worship. Specific rules, called "canons," for the Mass were organized and made universal for all Catholics. The Latin Vulgate was affirmed as the official translation of Scripture for the Catholic Church. Catholic schools for children were established, and a renewed focus was placed upon missions. Catholics were among the first to send missionaries to Latin America, Asia, India, and Africa. Today the pope continues to be one of the most important religious leaders in the world, and the Roman Catholic Church remains one of the oldest and strongest traditions represented within the Christian faith. An excellent example is Pope John Paul II, who emerged in the latter half of the twentieth century as a world leader able to speak with moral authority to a number of social issues.

The Pentecostal and Charismatic Movements

The teachings of the Holiness movement dominated the theological landscape of the United States in the nineteenth century. This paved the way for the *Pentecostal* movement, the most significant new Christian movement of the twentieth century. The modern Pentecostal movement began in 1901, in Topeka, Kansas, and has spread to every continent. The name "Pentecostal" is taken from a story in the book of Acts. There, the day of Pentecost refers to a time when the apostles received the Holy Spirit and spoke in various tongues. Pentecostalism emphasizes the power of the Holy Spirit and manifestations of that power. These include miracles, divine healing, and speaking in tongues. One of the most important of the early Pentecostal meetings took place in Los Angeles, at the Azusa Street revival (1906). William J. Seymour, an African-American Baptist Holiness preacher, was calling upon his followers to go beyond conversion into holiness and to be "baptized in the Holy Spirit." The Azusa Street experience drew large crowds and gathered attention from Christians throughout the United States. The Pentecostal revival soon spread throughout America and the world.

Today there are many Pentecostal denominations (over eleven thousand worldwide). Some of the best known are the Assemblies of God, the Church of the Four Square Gospel, and the Church of God in Christ. Millions of Christians participate in this form of Christianity, as well as in the related *charismatic* movement. Charismatic, or Neo-Pentecostal, Christianity emerged in the 1960s. It takes the emphasis of Pentecostals upon the Holy Spirit and spiritual gifts into the larger arena of established Christian denominations. Primarily a movement of the *laity,* it has become a significant influence in both Protestant and Roman Catholic churches around the globe.

Christianity and the Challenge of Diversity

As we have noted previously, Christianity is represented in a great diversity of cultures and communities. In part, this is due to the spread of the Christian faith through missionary activities. A missionary is one who goes on a mission of evangelism, seeking to spread the good news of Jesus Christ to others. Missionary efforts often involve living and working in foreign cultures, finding ways to translate the gospel message into a new social and cultural context. This outreach, carried on in the name of Christ, usually involves more than simply preaching the message of Christ and salvation. Modern mission workers are sent to assist communities with physical as well as spiritual needs. Missionaries often are trained in medicine, engineering, agriculture, or other specialties in demand in developing nations. They dig wells, build schools, advise farmers on crops, run health clinics, and meet other needs identified by the communities where they live. Modern missionaries bring with them a genuine desire to improve the physical as well as the spiritual lives of those whom they seek to evangelize.

However, the training and the cultural sensitivity that mark modern missions often were lacking in earlier centuries of missionary activity. In fact, there have been many cases in which missionary work served to advance the interests of European political power. European armies conquered peoples of Latin America, Africa, and Asia accompanied by merchants and representatives of the church. The cross and the sword were used to bring native populations under the influence and control of European political powers, often to the financial benefit of Europe. From the sixteenth to the twentieth centuries, the world was dominated by Western political powers, and the church was a significant force in the European colonization of conquered territories. Missionaries often associated Western cultural practices with Christian values and worked alongside the colonial powers to keep indigenous populations in control. Nevertheless, there were many missionaries and church representatives who advocated on behalf of the conquered peoples. For example, Catholics such as Antonio Montesinos, Bartolomé de Las Casas, and Francisco de Vitoria actively campaigned against the enslavement of native peoples in the Spanish colonies. Their actions resulted in the New Laws of the Indies, signed by Charles V in 1542. But for the most part, Western missionaries worked within the power structures of European colonies in Asia, Africa, and South America.

In contrast to missionary movements in Europe's "age of exploration," later efforts reflected increased cultural sensitivity and a growing appreciation of God-given diversity. The modern missionary movement began in the late eighteenth century, as Christians once again focused their attention on carrying the good news around the world. This time, the movement was to become both interdenominational and international, and believers went forward with a greater sense of respect and appreciation for the people whom they sought to evangelize. Two of the best-known examples are J. Hudson Taylor and David

**General Assemblies of
the World Council of Churches**

To date, the World Council of Churches has held eight assemblies to address ecumenical concerns. These are the dates, locations, and themes of the assemblies:

1948   *Amsterdam:* Man's Disorder and God's Reign

1954   *Evanston:* Racism and Colonialism

1961   *New Delhi:* Ecumenical Response to Human Suffering

1968   *Uppsala:* Economic and Social Justice; Population Control and Food Production and Distribution

1975   *Nairobi:* Interfaith Relations; Human Rights; Just, Participatory, and Sustainable Society; Nuclear Disarmament

1983   *Vancouver:* Jesus Christ, the Life of the World; Conciliar Process of Mutual Commitment for Justice, Peace, and Integrity of Creation

1991   *Canberra:* Come, Holy Spirit — Renew the Whole World

1998   *Zimbabwe:* Turn to God — Rejoice in Hope

Livingstone. Hudson Taylor traveled from his native England to carry the Christian gospel to China. His desire to spread the good news of God's love and forgiveness, rather than Western customs, led him to adopt the Chinese language, dress, and customs of his day. Although his approach initially was criticized, the idea that missionaries should live and dress like those whom they seek to reach for Christ soon became accepted. Legendary explorer David Livingstone worked for years among the African people as a missionary. He lived among the people, exploring the interior of the African continent and battling the slave trade. These examples underscore the change in attitude that had spread throughout the church as respect and understanding for cultural diversity increased.

Increasingly, the attention of the church also was directed to the divisions that had proliferated in the church across the centuries. During the nineteenth century, missionaries found that the divisions among Christians into many types and denominations hindered the spread of the gospel. Concerns such as this were addressed at the first International Missionary Council, which gathered in 1910 in Scotland. This was the beginning of the ecumenical movement, a worldwide effort to bring denominations together. After several years of planning (and the experience of two world wars), the World Council of Churches (WCC) was formed in 1948. Since its formation, 337 churches in 120 countries have joined the WCC in its attempt to promote Christian unity, renewal, witness, justice, and service to the world. Although not all of its decisions have been equally well received, it has provided a venue in which churches worldwide can cooperate in missions and come together in ministry and worship. The membership includes a large number of Orthodox and Protestant churches, and there is official dialogue between the Roman Catholics and the WCC.

In many ways, the Eastern Orthodox participation in the WCC renewed Western interest in the Orthodox tradition as a whole. Orthodox church leadership has become more visible and influential in the West, and in world affairs generally. The current spiritual head of Orthodox Christians, Bartholomew I, has been active in the leadership of the WCC prior to his ascension as ecumenical patriarch. With the fall of the Soviet Union, Bartholomew I began strengthening contact between the various Orthodox national churches in postcommunist Eastern Europe. In that environment, where the church had been restricted, suppressed, and even persecuted by the government of the Soviet Union, he provided guidance, leadership, and encouragement in the reestablishment of Orthodox churches. Like his religious contemporary Pope John Paul II, this ecumenical patriarch has recognized that the power of his position brings unique obligations and opportunities to speak to the moral and spiritual issues of life. Bartholomew I has taken a lead in raising awareness about ecological issues and in calling attention to the need for harmony between humankind and nature.

As the preceding examples demonstrate, Christian history is a mixed bag of triumphs and tragedies. As is the case with individual believers, the church sometimes is called to repent for its mistakes. This repentance can be a long time in coming because often it is difficult for Christians to see that they have done wrong when they believed they were in the right. It is a witness to the power of Jesus Christ that the Christian faith has prospered in the face of thoughtless, selfish, and even brutal actions taken in the name of the church. In part, this is because the Christian faith has shown itself to be a powerful source of hope and a model for justice and reconciliation. For example, in the tumultuous period surrounding the two world wars, colonies that had been controlled by Western political powers began to seek and to find independence from European control.

New Movements in Theology

The quest for liberation and the struggles for independence gave rise to *liberation theology*. From its origins in Latin America in the 1960s, liberation theology has reminded us that God remains firmly on the side of the poor and the oppressed. This movement has drawn the attention of the church to the political roots of oppression and injustice, and given a voice to the economically and politically powerless. The radical cry of liberation theology has been an important part of revolutionary movements in Latin America, Asia, and Africa. Other contemporary theological movements share concerns similar to those of liberation theology. *Black theology,* which arose among African Americans in North America, has spread to other countries and contexts. It too addresses issues of injustice and seeks to articulate a theology that reflects black experience and perspective. *Feminist theology* challenges the assumptions of theology shaped by patriarchy and negative views of women. In its many forms, liberation theology remains one of the most important theological forces of the twentieth century.

Another important development in the modern church took place in Rome starting in 1962. Very much influenced by the ecumenical movement, Pope John XXIII gathered Catholic bishops from around the globe to help the Roman Catholic Church meet the needs of the modern world. One of the most beloved and respected popes of all time, John XXIII saw the need to reform the church, and he called for a worldwide council of all Catholic bishops. The *Second Vatican Council* (1962–65) brought tremendous change to the Roman Catholic Church, especially in comparison to the much more conservative First Vatican Council (1869–70). The Catholic tradition expanded the place for the laity to participate in worship. The Mass, the center of Catholic worship, now could be said in local languages rather than in the previously required Latin. The pope was seen to teach and rule not alone, but in cooperation with all of the other bishops. Dialogue with Protestant and Orthodox Christians was established, and later it was expanded to include other world religions, including Judaism and Islam. As a result of this, the Roman Catholic pope and the Eastern Orthodox ecumenical patriarch of Constantinople have taken back the condemnation pronounced upon one another in the Great Schism of 1054. Although women still cannot be priests in the Roman Catholic Church, the place for leadership by women has greatly increased due to Vatican II. The worldwide character of the Roman Catholic Church is also better represented in the church hierarchy today, with bishops and cardinals being appointed from many more ethnic groups and from every continent.

In many ways, the diversity present in the church represents the challenge for Christians to understand themselves and the breadth of their calling in Christ. The early church quickly came to understand that the good news of Jesus Christ was intended for all humanity. The Reformation championed the idea that the Christian gospel is not the private domain of any one tradition. In our own time, the modern church has affirmed that the Christian faith is not the property of any single culture or race. Christians believe that the biblical message of forgiveness, salvation, and peace is a gift to all, and that it challenges the sin in every culture. The biblical message also calls followers of Jesus to be in union with the body of Christ. This teaching is central to the Christian understanding of the church, but it remains a difficult issue for believers around the world. Variations in worship style, church organizational structure, and leadership modes often have obscured the common elements of faith that different traditions share. Unnecessary division in the church has resulted from a number of human failings, including ignorance, misunderstanding, confusion, prejudice, unquestioning allegiance to organizational structures, political or racial ideology, and unwillingness to communicate between traditions. The church still needs to repent for the sins that continue to mark its existence in history. Despite this, Christians often have demonstrated a genuine willingness to gather across boundaries of church organizational structures. As the ecumenical movement has shown, the followers of Jesus Christ continue to desire, and to work for, unity. Although the Christian faith probably will never again come together under a single organizational banner, the beliefs that form the core of Christian doctrine increasingly serve as a common ground for unity among believers. Orthodox, Catholic, and Protestant Christians are called together by the life, death, and resurrection of Jesus Christ. This is the transforming message that meets them where they are and calls them into a new life of obedience to the God who created and loves all humankind.

Questions for Further Reflection

1. What changes did Protestantism bring to Christian religious practice?

2. Was the Protestant movement necessary in its day? Why or why not?

3. How did the Roman Catholic Church respond to the challenge of Protestantism?

4. Should the church be involved in leadership of ecological or social justice movements? Why or why not?

5. In your view, do the differences in today's churches make Christianity more or less attractive? Why?

Chapter 8

Christian Life and Thought

To this point, our encounter with Christianity has addressed basic components of the Christian faith. We have considered Christians' worship practices, their sacred text, and their greatest religious teacher. Yet for believers, understanding Christianity is more than information. Following Jesus Christ is first and foremost about a relationship with God. This relationship leads to a new way of life and a different understanding of human existence. In this last chapter we will discuss the most significant aspects of the Christian worldview, particularly moral and ethical teachings. Building upon your familiarity with Christian history and practice, we will expand our discussion to include theological beliefs that provide the basic elements of Christian life and thought. We begin our examination at the center: the gospel of Jesus Christ.

Christianity teaches that God has come in person to redeem a fallen human race. Christians believe in the good news that salvation is available now through Jesus Christ. This message of faith is a simple one in many ways. At the same time, there are a number of foundational beliefs upon which this faith is built. Christianity holds a belief in a holy God: the all-powerful, loving, just, and merciful creator. It affirms the view that human beings act in ways that are wrong, or morally blameworthy. This includes the understanding that these wrong actions or attitudes, called "sin," separate human beings from God. Fortunately, faith is also the acceptance that God has made a way for human beings to be reconciled spiritually with God, in the person of Jesus Christ. This person, God *incarnate,* gave his life for all who wish to be reunited with God. Through the sacrifice of Jesus Christ and his resurrection from the dead, fallen human beings have new life available to them.

This new life involves more than simply concurring with certain ideas or adopting a particular philosophy. It means placing trust in God for every aspect of life and learning to be obedient. To follow Christ is to embrace inward transformation. In this process, human character is slowly reshaped into God's holy likeness. Love, kindness, compassion, joy, humility, and patience become part of this new inward nature. But Christian Scripture also teaches that "faith without works is dead" (James 2:17). This means that the inward changes will be evident in one's actions. Believers are commanded to respond as Jesus Christ would to all of life's situations. Christians believe that it is possible to do this only through the power of God's Holy Spirit. Every Christian is called to live in service and obedience to God. Every aspect of our human existence — our relationships, our possessions, even our very thoughts — should be subject to God. For this reason, Christians should not separate the various areas of life into categories of "holy" and "unholy." Rather, all work and living should be done in such a way that honors God and brings glory to the name of Jesus. Commitment to Christ means that all aspects of life have value, and his presence in one's life can make even the most mundane task a sacred and holy experience. According to the Second Vatican Council, "Worshipping everywhere by our holy actions, the laity [ordinary believers] consecrate the world itself to God, everywhere offering worship by the holiness of our lives" (*Lumen Gentium,* 34). These are beautiful words. But what do they mean? What does it mean to live a holy life?

In answering this question, Christians look to four sources: Scripture, tradition, experience, and reason. Scripture is the

Bible, their sacred text. Tradition is the wisdom and teaching of the Christian faith, passed on from previous generations. Experience is personal insight gained from encounters with God and the world. Reason is the rational faculty that God has given all human beings, used to reflect upon the meaning of Scripture, tradition, and experience. Among these various norms, Scripture plays a guiding role. First, Scripture interprets itself. You will recall that the Bible is a "book of books," and each passage must be interpreted in light of what the whole Bible teaches. Second, Scripture informs tradition. Tradition brings us wisdom from the past, wisdom that has its source in the God of Scripture. Third, Scripture validates and judges our experience. Human experience is subject to the limitations of our finite existence. Scripture gives us categories for understanding spiritual encounters. Fourth, Scripture guides reason. Christians believe that the Bible gives insight into God's character and will, and this helps in making informed judgments and taking appropriate actions. In the context of all these sources, the Bible gives a vision of life and a grand story of all creation in which all people can find hope, joy, and peace.

Christian Ethics

Christians turn to the grand biblical narrative and vision as a guide for human life. The sacred Scriptures, then, are basic to the formation of Christian ethics. Ethics is the study of human character and conduct and the nature of moral principles and obligations. Although ethics is a broad discipline that is beyond the scope of this book, we do want to survey some significant Christian teachings in this area. In particular, we will look at the Ten Commandments, which are in many ways a summary of Old Testament ethics. Then we will look to Jesus' teachings and the two commandments that he affirmed above all others.

Moving from biblical standards of behavior to questions of personal character, we will look at the classic Christian virtues. We then will look at character in the context of Jesus Christ and his famous teaching known as the Beatitudes.

The Ten Commandments are found in two places in the Bible: Exodus 20 and Deuteronomy 5. There are small variations between these two versions, but no substantial differences (although different traditions do number the commandments in different ways). In the Exodus version, God has just rescued his people from Egypt, "the house of bondage" (Exodus 20:2). Because of divine love and goodness, God is now making a covenant with his people (Deuteronomy 5:2–3). A covenant is a solemn agreement between two parties, and here God promises to be the Lord God, protector of Israel. Israel then promises to be obedient to God. As Moses says of obedience to God's commandments, "Hear therefore, O Israel, and observe them diligently, so that it may go well with you, and so that you may multiply greatly in a land flowing with milk and honey, as the Lord, the God of your ancestors, has promised you" (Deuteronomy 6:3). The purpose of the law, then, is to bring blessing to the people of God.

The first commandment says, "You shall have no other gods." The one true Lord of the universe demands the worship that is due to him alone. He is the creator, and will not allow the worship of anything created. Christians believe that human beings are to love God, to worship and honor God, and to find in God the true meaning of their lives. This means that possessions, jobs, and even families are to be viewed as gifts from God, given by the creator. As precious as these things are, Christians believe that they must not be allowed to become more important than God, who gives them. This approach to valued things applies not only to individual believers, but also to the whole people of God. Christians are joined together as one in Christ, unified in his life, death, and resurrection. Remember that union with Christ

The Ten Commandments

1. You shall have no other gods.

2. You shall not worship graven images.

3. You shall not take the name of the Lord your God in vain.

4. Remember the Sabbath day, and keep it holy.

5. Honor your father and your mother.

6. You shall not murder.

7. You shall not commit adultery.

8. You shall not steal.

9. You shall not bear false witness.

10. You shall not covet.

commits his followers to worship God as a group, not merely as individuals. This commandment is the key to all the rest. A right relationship with God, based on faith in him, is the foundation of the truly moral and the truly happy life. Christ's followers teach that no created thing should be the ultimate purpose of human existence, not even loved ones and families. Only God, the one who creates and sustains humankind, deserves worship.

The second commandment continues the theme of the first. "You shall not worship graven images." God is invisible, and since he alone is to be worshiped, no carving or image of God, or of anything else, should be made for that purpose. Of course, Christians have always been involved in art. Painting, sculpture, and architecture are wonderful media of artistic creation and spiritual expression, and skills and gifts in these areas should be cultivated in all who seek to create beautiful works of art, which should be cherished. The second commandment does not forbid the creation of works of art; rather, it forbids the worship of anything but God alone.

The third commandment says, "You shall not take the name of the Lord your God in vain." The sense of this commandment is that human beings are not to seek to manipulate God, because we now have this special relationship in a covenant. We know the true name of God ("Yahweh," in Hebrew). God, in humility and love, has revealed himself to us. The third commandment forbids us from taking advantage of God's goodness. Instead, our proper response to divine goodness and mercy is to respect God and the relationship we have with him. For those who truly love God, *blasphemy* (the misuse of God's name, or of the name of Jesus Christ) is a serious moral problem. The use of God's name as a curse word or to justify wicked deeds is symptomatic of a heart turned toward evil.

The fourth commandment says, "Remember the Sabbath day, and keep it holy." Like the first three commandments, this one concerns the human relationship with God. Labor is a gift of God by which we earn our daily bread. Through labor, human beings participate in the creativity of God. But God has not intended humans for work alone. Work is an expression of the creativity and talent that God has given to each person. It should never be made into a kind of god. Rather, we are created for a relationship with God and for holy fellowship or communion with each other. The Sabbath day was created to remind people of this fact. The seventh day, Saturday, was holy to God in ancient Israel. That was a day when work was forbidden so that people could rest in God. It was a holy day, a day of worship. Because Jesus rose from the dead on Sunday, Christians have transferred their day of worship to Sunday.

The fifth commandment moves from our relationship with God to our relationship with other people. In biblical ethics, God comes first. If we have a right relationship with God, it creates the context in which the rest of our lives can flow with peace, love, and inner strength. Next comes the family. "Honor your father and your mother," says the fifth commandment. When God created Adam and Eve and called them to be one, this established the foundation of the human family (Genesis 2). The commandment "be fruitful and multiply" (Genesis 1:28) reflects the fact that people are created in the image of God. Bringing forth new life in love, the married couple participates in the creativity of God. Thus, marriage is a holy covenant between the couple and God, the author of sexuality. The fifth commandment calls upon children to respect this role that God has given to parents. Of course, this does not allow for the abuse or neglect of children; parents likewise must respect and care for their children (Proverbs 22:6; Ephesians 6:4). By extension, established political authorities likewise should be honored (see Romans 13:1). But although Christianity respects local government, it also knows that these powers can be abused. The highest loyalty always must go to the ultimate ruler, God.

The sixth commandment turns to human beings in general, and sanctifies our very lives. "You shall not murder [kill]" draws a boundary around the life of every individual. Elsewhere the Bible says, "Do not slay the innocent and the righteous" (Exodus 23:7). The life of every human being is to be respected as a creation and gift of God that is not ours to take away from another. The only apparent exceptions to this are found in the Old Testament, which allows for killing in the cases of capital punishment and war, although many interpreters consider such killing to be different from murder (note the alternative translation "kill" in the sixth commandment, given above). The highest expression of this commandment is found in the teachings of Jesus. He said to his followers, "Love your enemies and pray for those who persecute you" (Matthew 5:44).

The seventh commandment focuses again on the family. "Do not commit adultery." Adultery occurs when married people break their covenant with each other, and have sex with someone other than their spouse. Since the love between man and woman in marriage reflects the nature of God, God forbids sexual encounters outside of marriage. Sex was created to intensify a lifelong, loving union — a holy marriage. Christians teach that self-control is a key virtue. We should learn to control our passions and lusts, and not give in to every temptation and pleasure (see 1 Thessalonians 4:3–5). In the area of sexuality, although sex is a created good, it is not the most important thing about a person.

We need to place sex in its proper place, which for biblical ethics is the marriage bed. Our sexuality is an essential part of our personal identity, and Christians call everyone to sexual chastity — that is, the proper use and control of sexual intimacy. Anyone, married or single, can be chaste. The chaste single person is celibate (abstains from sexual encounters). The chaste married person respects the commitment and the sexual intimacy of his or her spouse. Therefore, adultery is forbidden in Scripture. This shows once again the importance of family life to God.

The eighth commandment returns to the general human population. "You shall not steal." God had given the whole of the earth to the whole human race (Genesis 1:26–30). In order to provide for the security of families and individuals, the possession of personal property must also be respected. But ownership of property is not an absolute right. Government regulates property ownership, for example. More importantly, all of the earth belongs to God (Psalm 24:1); we are but stewards and caretakers of God's world. For this reason, Christians have taught that using the goods of others to protect our own lives (or those of our family) is not morally wrong.

The ninth commandment turns from ownership of property to relationships in community. In human communication, truth is essential. Therefore, "You shall not bear false witness." Although this commandment originally applied to the courtroom, it extends to a general principle of honesty. Since God is true (John 3:33; Romans 3:4), human beings are called to a life of truth telling. Lying undermines the gathering and flourishing of human community. Christians respect the truth, and so they should seek it and stand up for it. They should not hide the truth, even painful truth about themselves. In the Bible, light is a common metaphor for truth. In the light of God, Christians are also called to be the light of the world (Matthew 5:14).

The temptation to lie or to steal often has its root in a desire for what we do not have. Thus, the tenth commandment says, "You shall not covet." Envy and lust for material wealth or sexual pleasure can be very destructive. Christians are called to be thankful for "daily bread" (see Matthew 6:11) and to trust in God to meet daily needs. An excessive or improper desire for wealth, power, or pleasure can block their relationship with God, and keep them from loving their neighbors and living a Christlike life.

The Greatest Commandments

1. You shall love the Lord your God with all your heart, and with all your soul, and with all your might (Deuteronomy 6:5).

2. You shall love your neighbor as yourself (Leviticus 19:18).

Love and Christian Virtue

Loving one's "neighbor" is a central theme in Christian ethics. When Jesus was asked which was the most important of the commandments, he answered, " 'You shall love the Lord your God with all your heart, and with all your soul, and with all your mind.' This is the greatest and first commandment. And the second is like it: 'You shall love your neighbor as yourself.' On these two commandments hang all the Law and the Prophets" (Matthew 22:37–39). Jesus here is quoting from the Old Testament (Deuteronomy 6:5; Leviticus 19:18). He is pointing to the heart of biblical ethics. Christian ethics is not simply about outward appearances. To see biblical ethics as simply a list of one "you shall not" after another is a major mistake. Rather, Christian ethics is about morality from the inside out. Once a person's inward, spiritual self has been reconciled with God through Jesus Christ, the rest of his or her moral life will begin to shape up over time. And the inside orientation of the mind (or soul) must be love: the love of God over all things, and the love of neighbor.

Christian love is not simply an emotion or feeling. Rather, this love is an active willingness to work on the behalf of others. It is love in the way that parents love their children. In love we see the need in others' lives and seek to meet it from our own strengths. Love is an attitude of the soul in which we are willing to be a servant to others. But this is not the same as being a doormat! We do not give in to the evil and sin in the human heart. Rather, we seek the good in others and help to nurture that goodness. This is seen in the book of 1 Corinthians, where the apostle Paul sends the church one of the most beautiful meditations on love ever written:

> If I speak with the tongues of mortals and of angels, but do not have love, I am a noisy gong or a clanging cymbal.

And if I have prophetic powers, and understand all mysteries and all knowledge, and if I have all faith, so as to remove mountains, but do not have love, I am nothing. If I give away all my possessions, and if I hand over my body so that I may boast, but do not have love, I gain nothing. Love is patient; love is kind; love is not envious or boastful or arrogant or rude. It does not insist on its own way; it is not irritable or resentful; it does not rejoice in wrongdoing, but rejoices in the truth. It bears all things, believes all things, hopes all things, endures all things. Love never ends. (1 Corinthians 13:1–8)

In order to help the soul on the long journey to God and in the difficult task of loving one's neighbors, Christian tradition has developed an ethical teaching that focuses on *virtues,* which are habits of the soul, or character traits, that lead us to good deeds. Bad habits, on the other hand, are called *vices,* and they lead us to evil deeds. Virtues guide us into doing what is good. A virtuous person, then, is a good person. Virtues, like other habits, are built into one's character over a long period of time. The Christian teachings on moral character affirm that cultivation and development of the human soul takes commitment, practice, and diligence. In addition to a focus on rules and behavior, Christianity has developed an ethics of virtue. These virtues are derived from biblical teachings, and they summarize the teachings of the Bible concerning a holy character in the eyes of God.

Among these "habits of the heart," seven are considered the most important. These are the three theological virtues, and the four *cardinal virtues.* The word "cardinal" comes from a Latin word that means "hinge." These virtues are cardinal in that they are key or pivotal for growth in good moral character. The first three are called "theological" because they have God as their focus. The other four virtues, which can be found in many

> **The Christian Virtues**
>
> *Theological:*
>   Faith
>   Hope
>   Love
>
> *Cardinal:*
>   Wisdom (Prudence)
>   Self-control (Temperance)
>   Courage (Fortitude)
>   Honesty (Justice)

philosophies and religions, focus upon proper relationship with one's neighbors.

The three theological virtues are faith, hope, and love. The apostle Paul called these virtues the greatest of all spiritual gifts; and the greatest of these, he wrote, is love (1 Corinthians 13:13). Paul here is reflecting the ethical teachings of his master, Jesus. Love is the greatest of all the virtues. Love is the proper motivation for ethical action toward our fellow human beings, and love of God aligns our lives in the right direction, toward God. This is because, according to Scripture, God is love. "Whoever does not love does not know God, for God is love," writes John the elder apostle (1 John 4:8). Love is the greatest of virtues because God's love powers the very heart of the universe. Love for God is therefore essential to finding the true meaning of life.

Faith is closely connected with love. Faith is a virtue of trust in God, even when things are looking gloomy. In the most famous of the psalms, the poet declares, "Even though I walk through the darkest valley, I fear no evil; for you are with me" (Psalm 23:4). Faith is an active trust in the goodness, mercy,

and plan of God. But faith is more than that. Faith also includes belief — that is, accepting that certain things are true,
even if they cannot be proven. For example, Christian faith includes the beliefs that God created the universe and that Jesus
is the Son of God. To trust in God also means to trust that certain things are true about God. So, for example, Christians trust
that God keeps his promises. Yet faith requires even more. True
faith results in a new way of life, in striving to please God in
every way. Faith results in action; if not, then it is not the true
virtue of faith. For example, Paul writes in his letter to the Romans that "the righteous shall live by faith," and that his goal
was to "bring about the obedience of faith" in people (Romans
1:17, 5). Notice that for Paul, faith is something that people
live, something that brings about obedience to the commandments. To summarize: the virtue of faith is trust and belief that
brings about obedience to God. The importance of faith in the
heart of the Christian is second only to love.

Because of faith in God and love for God, the Christian also
has hope in God. Christian hope assumes faith, since it is hope
in God and God's promises. Christians have hope in the future
because they know that God is the Lord of history. God eventually will bring peace, justice, and harmony to the whole world,
destroying the forces of evil and sin. Christians hope in God,
not in human powers, for the future. Yet this is not just a "pie in
the sky by and by" kind of hope. It is grounded in the reality of
the ministry, suffering, death, and resurrection of Jesus (Romans
5:1–21; 8:1–39). It is due in part to this hope that Christians are
free to love the needy without fear. In faith and hope, Christians
are empowered to love their neighbors. Of course, this work is
not possible apart from the Holy Spirit (Romans 15:13).

People cannot fully develop these three theological virtues on
their own. The church teaches that true growth in Christian
virtue is possible only through the work of God in the human
soul. God the Holy Spirit gives the grace and strength needed

to live out of love, faith, and hope. Through a relationship with God, people grow in virtue. But that is not all. Christians also teach that community and practice are essential to growth in moral character. For this, human beings need the church — that is, the fellowship of others who are seeking to live according to the same moral standards. Christians can assist one another with honesty, support, and prayer as they seek holiness of life. It is also in the context of community that true character is revealed. Believers point out that when they are among those who know them and who are familiar with their character in unguarded moments, they must acknowledge their true nature. The steady spiritual growth that Christ's redemptive love provides is easily measured in the day-to-day interactions with those who know us best.

Like the Ten Commandments, the virtues are ordered first to God and then to neighbor. The three theological virtues have direct application to God, and from that divine connection, faith, hope, and love look to the world. The four cardinal virtues are oriented more toward everyday life, but they also affect one's relationship to God and to the church. These cardinal virtues are ones that other religions and philosophies also hold to. They are wisdom, self-control, courage, and honesty. Here, we have listed these virtues using their modern names, but in classical Christian texts they bear older names: prudence (wisdom), temperance (self-control), fortitude (courage), and justice (honesty.)

Prudence, or wisdom, is the chief of the cardinal virtues. By wisdom we understand how we can make our way morally in a difficult world. Becoming wise is not easy. Even though they seek to love God with all they are and do, Christians know that growth in morality, especially in these troubled times, takes insight, thoughtfulness, and good sense. The book of Proverbs begins with a call to seek out this wisdom: "The fear of the Lord is the beginning of wisdom, but fools despise wisdom and instruction" (Proverbs 1:7). Here, "fear" means a sense of awe before the majesty of God, not actual terror or fright. The worship of God in one's heart is the foundation of moral insight, and the root cause of wisdom.

After the virtue of wisdom comes temperance, or self-control. It is unfortunate that temperance has come to mean self-control only in regard to the consumption of alcoholic beverages. Temperance used to mean moderation and self-control in all areas of life. Christianity teaches that a wise person will use God's good earth, but not abuse it. It is possible to overindulge in many things: food, sports, computers, television, movies, sex. Almost anything pleasant and pleasurable can be abused if human beings engage in it to excess. The virtue of wisdom teaches self-control in these areas of fun. Life should be enjoyable, but Christians have long cautioned that too much of a good thing can be harmful to body and soul. In keeping with the Ten Commandments, human beings must not place ultimate meaning and hope in anything less than God himself. Life is meant to be lived to the glory of God, not to the excess of pleasure.

Although self-control is important, there are times when we need to assert ourselves. The life of goodness and love requires fortitude, or courage, to live. The world too often runs over those who are willing to serve others at their own expense. Jesus himself, after all, was crucified by the very people he came to save. Why should his followers expect any different treatment? Courage is not foolishness, but the strength to stand up for what is right. The true hero is the one who defends the innocent, who stands up for justice, when everyone else would look the other way. Of course, courage without wisdom and love can be self-righteous, or just plain stupid. But courage in the face of evil is necessary for those who seek to live a life of virtue.

The last cardinal virtue is justice, or honesty. We live in a world in which concern for image and power overshadows concern for truth and honesty. Of course, no one wants to be known as a liar or a cheat, and yet lying and cheating are among the most common human vices. Those who follow Jesus Christ are called to lay aside such behavior and to value purity of heart and mind. This often leads Christians into conflict with the expectations and practices of the surrounding culture. Since its inception, the Christian faith has been expressed in the lives of believers who look to Jesus Christ as the standard for what is good and right. Their faith teaches that the power to live in accordance with God's standards comes from the Holy Spirit, who is present with them every day.

These seven virtues tell a great deal about the goal of Christian character. The most famous summary of Jesus' teachings on virtue and love is found in Matthew's Gospel. Here, in the Sermon on the Mount, Jesus challenges the listener to examine the true nature of power and goodness (Matthew 5–7). Jesus has called his disciples together, and now he teaches them on a hilltop near the Sea of Galilee. As he begins his teachings, he describes the kind of person who best pleases God. This is summed up in nine sayings known as the Beatitudes, from a Latin word meaning "blessed." They describe the kind of person who is blessed by God. Each sentence begins with "Blessed are those.... " Jesus is explaining, then, the kind of person who is blessed by God with true spiritual joy. In the rest of this sermon, Jesus focuses on character or the soul. The sermon is not about behaviors or rules, although often it has been interpreted in that way. Instead, Jesus sets forth the kind of character that pleases God, and that God will bless in his kingdom. The Beatitudes set a very high standard. Those who are blessed by God are not concerned for material wealth; rather, they are poor "in spirit." As Jesus says later in his sermon, "You cannot serve God and money" (Matthew 6:24). Those who please God and share God's compassion for the world will mourn the destruction and suffering that evil brings. But mourning hearts will be comforted when they witness the future reign, or kingdom, of

The Beatitudes
(Matthew 5:1–12)

When Jesus saw the crowds, he went up the mountain; and after he sat down, his disciples came to him. Then he began to speak, and taught them, saying:

"Blessed are the poor in spirit, for theirs is the kingdom of heaven.

"Blessed are those who mourn, for they will be comforted.

"Blessed are the meek, for they will inherit the earth.

"Blessed are those who hunger and thirst for righteousness, for they will be filled.

"Blessed are the merciful, for they will receive mercy.

"Blessed are the pure in heart, for they will see God.

"Blessed are the peacemakers, for they will be called children of God.

"Blessed are those who are persecuted for righteousness' sake, for theirs is the kingdom of heaven.

"Blessed are you when people revile you and persecute you and utter all kinds of evil against you falsely on my account. Rejoice and be glad, for your reward is great in heaven."

God. God also exalts the humble and the meek rather than the arrogant and the powerful.

Humility is another important virtue that Jesus exemplified. Jesus also calls us to hunger and thirst for justice and righteousness. Justice is what we seek in the world, and righteousness is what we seek in ourselves. The Greek word used for "righteousness" in Matthew 5:6 includes both concepts. Mercy is another quality that Christ's followers should hunger for in their own character. The quality of being "pure in heart," of having pure intentions and motives, may be the most difficult of all to attain. Yet Jesus promises that people who do so "will see God." Seeking mercy and justice, the true Christian also will seek peace, and will be known as one who makes peace with others. Such a person, who is loving, humble, and honest, is bound to be persecuted. Jesus is well aware of the need for courage to follow God's ways. The Beatitudes begin and end with the promise of God's rule and realm in the future (the kingdom of heaven), when those who seek God's will on earth will be restored. The greatest of all blessings is a close relationship with God in this life and in the next. These blessings are promised to those who follow the difficult path of peace and love.

Jesus sets a high standard for living as a Christian. When we study the Ten Commandments, the two greatest commandments, the seven virtues, and the Beatitudes, the scope and depth of Christian ethical standards seem overwhelming. We can be thankful that Christians are not expected to achieve these goals through their own power. The Christian faith teaches that the power of God's Holy Spirit has been sent by Christ. In John's Gospel, Jesus, after his resurrection, breathes on his followers and says, "Receive the Holy Spirit" (John 20:22). In the book of Acts, the coming of the Holy Spirit is the powerful event that begins the ministry and spread of the church (Acts 2). The Christian is not left alone to struggle for holiness of character. Rather, the Spirit of God dwells within the Christian's mind and soul, guiding, empowering, forgiving, and loving each one toward holiness. For this reason, the Bible calls the Spirit of Christ (or the Spirit of God) the Spirit of Holiness — that is, the Holy Spirit (see Romans 1:4–6).

As we noted previously, the fellowship of believers provides another resource for living the Christian life. Here, the importance of the church's role as a community of faith becomes apparent. As Christians gather together on the Sabbath day, they find the support, instruction, and encouragement necessary to grow in the life of faith. This time of worship and fellowship is a drawing together of Christ's body. Together they celebrate the presence of God in their midst as they worship. Christians throughout the centuries have realized the value of community in the Christian journey. Here, Christians learn what every family must learn: to be kind and compassionate, to be patient and forgiving, to share joy and sorrow, and to take comfort in being loved despite our faults. Such practices of common devotion strengthen the soul for the struggles and joys of Christian existence.

Christian Theology

When Christians begin to dig deeper into their understanding of the Christian life, they find God at work. Christian ethics is not possible without the work of God in the people of God. In the Bible and in the teachings of the church, theology and ethics always have gone together. Theology is the study of God. The knowledge of God is central to a godly (moral, Christian) life, and a godly life is based upon a relationship with, and knowledge of, God. Christians early on understood the value of well-articulated theology, as well as good morality. For this reason, a single chapter can hardly do justice to Christian morality and theology. However, the material is of such significance that we will provide an overview as a starting point for later studies on your own. One tried-and-true method for summarizing Christian theology is to return to a very early statement of Christian belief, the Apostles' Creed. You will recall from an earlier chapter that this creed arose from the worship practices of the early church. Those who wished to be baptized memorized it as part of their Christian training. It is still widely used in worship services today, and is accepted by virtually all Christian churches as a basic statement of faith. The Apostles' Creed has three paragraphs, or "articles," which talk about the three Persons within the one God. Like Jews and Muslims, Christians believe that there is only one God, who created all things, the "creator of heaven and earth." However, unlike Jews and Muslims, who historically are connected with Christianity, Christians affirm that although God's being is one, the one being of God has three personal centers of existence. The three Persons of God are in unity, making up the one being of God. The personhood of the infinite God, according to Christians, is more complex than human, finite personhood. God is three "persons" in one being. These three are named in the Bible and in the Apostles' Creed as God the Father, God the Son, and God the Holy Spirit.

The first article of the Apostles' Creed focuses on God the Father, who is the creator of heaven and earth. That God is "Father" indicates that he is the creator of all people, and the one whom they should worship and love. The church believes that God, as spiritual Parent, seeks what is best for us and wants to have a personal relationship with each of his children. In theory, God also might be called our heavenly "Mother," but this language for God, although being used more frequently now in contemporary Christianity, is quite rare in the Bible and in the older traditions of the church. In any case, Christians always have believed that God, without actually being either male or female, has all the best qualities of loving human fathers and mothers.

The second article of the Apostles' Creed is the longest. It summarizes the story of God the Son, the Father's "only son, our Lord." This belief about Jesus separated the early Christians from the philosophies and religions that surrounded them. This, of course, made the emphasis on him very important.

The Apostles' Creed
(late second century)

- I believe in God, the Father Almighty, creator of heaven and earth.

- I believe in Jesus Christ, his only son, our Lord. He was conceived by the power of the Holy Spirit and born to the Virgin Mary. He suffered under Pontius Pilate, was crucified, died, and was buried. He descended to the dead. On the third day, he rose again. He ascended into heaven and is seated at the right hand of the Father. He will come again to judge the living and the dead.

- I believe in the Holy Spirit, the holy catholic church, the communion of saints, the forgiveness of sins, the resurrection of the body, and the life everlasting.

Christians believe that God personally came to save them in the human being Jesus of Nazareth. God the Son was born of the Virgin Mary, and he suffered and died like other mortals. Yet in this suffering, Jesus became the savior of the world, "the Lord." He even went down to the realm of "the dead" (or to "hell," as some translations have it), which is the place where the spirits of people go after they die. But death was not the end of the story of Jesus. He rose from the dead, and thus he was able to conquer both sin and death. Christians also look toward the future of Christ, when he will establish the full and final kingdom of God. Until then, he dwells with the Father in heaven.

Although Jesus Christ dwells with God, he is not absent from the church on earth. God the Holy Spirit lives in and with the people of God. As we mentioned previously, the Holy Spirit empowers the believer to live a good life, one that gives glory to God. The Holy Spirit is God present in services of worship, in service to the poor and the outcast, in the life of prayer, and in one's soul. In the third article of the Apostles' Creed, the early Christians focused upon the work of the Holy Spirit in four areas. The first is the "holy catholic [universal] church" and the "communion of saints." In fellowship as the one, universal body of Christ, the early Christians discovered the fellowship of God the Holy Spirit. They accepted the idea that even dead Christians are part of the "communion of saints [holy people]" in God.

Essential to this spiritual fellowship is the "forgiveness of sins." Christianity teaches that as human beings repent of evil deeds and accept the gift of God's forgiveness made in and through Jesus, the Holy Spirit cleans up their souls. Human sins are forgiven, and new power and joy become available through the Spirit. The Holy Spirit continues within people a powerful relationship with God, which is the foundation of Christian life. This life, however, does not end even in death. Rather, the promise of God is that human beings will be given new and immortal bodies. The Apostles' Creed ends with an affirmation of faith in the face of death: the resurrection of our bodies, and life forever with God. This is an echo of promises made by Jesus in the Beatitudes: the meek will inherit the earth, and the pure in heart will see God.

In this last chapter we have given a very brief overview of the elements of Christianity that Christians hold most dear. A deep and personal relationship with God, lived on a daily basis, leads the believer into a more holy life and into a thirst for knowledge of God. Christian ethics and Christian theology both find their center and purpose in the worship and love of God. In a personal and spiritual relationship with the infinite One who made heaven and earth — God the Father, God the Son, and God the Holy Spirit — and in the worship and love of this one God, we find the true heart of Christianity.

Questions for Further Reflection

1. What role do doctrines play in the practice of religious faith?

2. How does the practice of a religion help us understand the teachings and doctrines of that religion?

3. What role does the Bible play in Christian life?

4. What are some of the key principles of Christian ethics?

5. What are some of the key principles of Christian theology? Which ones do you find difficult to believe, and why?

Suggestions for Further Reading

General

Bajis, Jordan. *Common Ground: An Introduction to Eastern Christianity.* Kansas City: Light and Life, 1991.

Lewis, C. S. *Mere Christianity.* New York: Macmillan, 1952.

McGrath, Alister. *An Introduction to Christianity.* Oxford: Blackwell, 1997.

Ratzinger, Joseph. *Introduction to Christianity.* San Francisco: Ignatius Press, 1990.

Stott, John R. W. *Basic Christianity.* Downers Grove, Ill.: InterVarsity Press, 1976.

Jesus and the Bible

Brown, Raymond, et al., eds. *The New Jerome Bible Handbook.* Collegeville, Minn.: Liturgical Press, 1992.

———. *The New Jerome Biblical Commentary.* Englewood Cliffs, N.J.: Prentice-Hall, 1990.

Freedman, David Noel, ed. *Eerdmans Dictionary of the Bible.* Grand Rapids, Mich.: Eerdmans, 2000.

May, H. G., ed. *Oxford Bible Atlas.* Oxford: Oxford University Press, 1985.

O'Collins, Gerald. *What Are They Saying about Jesus?* New York: Paulist Press, 1983.

Theissen, Gerd. *The Shadow of the Galilean.* Philadelphia: Fortress Press, 1987.

Wright, N. T. *Who Was Jesus?* Grand Rapids, Mich.: Eerdmans, 1993.

Church History

Bellitto, Christopher M. *The General Councils: A History of Twenty-one Church Councils from Nicaea to Vatican II.* Mahwah, N.J.: Paulist Press, 2002.

Gonzales, Justo. *The Story of Christianity.* 2 vols. San Francisco: HarperSanFrancisco, 1985.

Irvin, Dale, and Scott Sundquist. *History of the World Christian Movement.* 2 vols. Maryknoll, N.Y.: Orbis Books, 2001–4.

Livingstone, Elizabeth, ed. *Oxford Dictionary of the Christian Church.* 3d ed. Oxford: Oxford University Press, 1997.

McGonigle, Thomas, and J. F. Quigley. *A History of the Christian Tradition.* 2 vols. New York: Paulist Press, 1996.

Noll, Mark. *Turning Points.* Grand Rapids, Mich.: Baker Books, 1997.

Norris, Frederick W. *Christianity: A Short Global History.* Oxford: Oneworld, 2002.

Olson, Roger. *The Story of Christian Theology.* Downers Grove, Ill.: InterVarsity Press, 2001.

Stark, Rodney. *The Rise of Christianity: How the Obscure, Marginal Jesus Movement Became the Dominant Religious Force in the Western World in a Few Centuries.* San Francisco: HarperSanFrancisco, 1997.

Prayer and Worship

Bradshaw, Paul, ed. *The New SCM Dictionary of Liturgy and Worship.* London: SCM, 2002. U.S.A.: *The New Westminster Dictionary of Liturgy and Worship.* Louisville: Westminster John Knox, 2003.

Carretto, Carlo. *Letters from the Desert.* Maryknoll, N.Y.: Orbis Books, 2002.

Dix, Dom Gregory. *The Shape of the Liturgy.* New York: Continuum, 2000.

Fink, Peter, ed. *New Dictionary of Sacramental Worship.* Collegeville, Minn.: Michael Glazier, 1990.

Forrester, Duncan B., et al. *Encounter with God: An Introduction to Christian Worship and Practise.* Edinburgh: T. & T. Clark, 1996.

Foster, Richard. *Celebration of Discipline.* San Francisco: HarperSanFrancisco, 1988.

Klauser, Theodor. *A Short History of the Western Liturgy.* Oxford: Oxford University Press, 1979.

Peterson, David. *Engaging with God: A Biblical Theology of Worship.* Grand Rapids, Mich.: Eerdmans, 1993.

Schmemann, Alexander. *Introduction to Liturgical Theology.* Crestwood, N.Y.: St. Valdimir's Seminary Press, 2001.

Christian Theology

The Catechism of the Catholic Church. Washington, D.C.: U.S. Catholic Conference, 2000.

Hanson, Bruce. *Introduction to Christian Theology.* Minneapolis: Fortress, 1990.

McGrath, Alister. *Christian Theology: An Introduction.* 3d ed. Oxford: Blackwell, 2001.

Meyendorff, John. *The Orthodox Church.* Crestwood, N.Y.: St. Vladimir's Seminary Press, 1996.

Nichol, Adrian. *The Shape of Catholic Theology.* Collegeville, Minn.: Liturgical Press, 1991.

O'Collins, Gerald, and Edward Farrugia. *A Concise Dictionary of Theology.* Mahwah, N.J.: Paulist Press, 2000.

Christian Ethics

Connors, Russell, and T. T. McCormick. *Character, Choices, and Community: The Three Faces of Christian Ethics.* New York: Paulist Press, 1998.

Gutiérrez, Gustavo. *The God of Life.* Maryknoll, N.Y.: Orbis Books, 1991.

Hauerwas, Stanley. *The Peaceable Kingdom.* Notre Dame, Ind.: University of Notre Dame Press, 1983.

Himes, Kenneth. *Responses to 101 Questions on Catholic Social Teachings.* New York: Paulist Press, 2001.

Wilkens, Steve. *Beyond Bumper Sticker Ethics: An Introduction to Theories of Right and Wrong.* Downers Grove, Ill.: InterVarsity Press, 1995.

Yoder, John Howard. *The Politics of Jesus.* Grand Rapids, Mich.: Eerdmans, 1994.

Glossary

*Note: All terms in this Glossary
are also found in the Index.*

A.D. From Latin, *Anno Domini,* meaning "in the year of the Lord." It is used in dates to indicate years after the birth of Jesus; now often being replaced by "C.E." for "Common Era."

Advent. The four-week season that begins the Christian year, which starts in November or December. Advent is the season of waiting for the coming of the Messiah, Jesus, and ends on Christmas Day.

Anabaptists. A term meaning "rebaptizers." It was used to describe and define certain Christians during the Reformation who rejected the practice of infant baptism in favor of a "believer's baptism" as adults.

Anglican. A communion of churches stemming from the Church of England, which broke from Rome and the pope during the Reformation; also called Episcopalian.

Apocalyptic. Symbolic Jewish stories having to do with the cosmic battle between good and evil, and the final victory of God. The best-known apocalyptic text is the Book of Revelation, also called the Apocalypse.

Apologists. Early Christian thinkers and writers whose task was to present a reasoned defense of the faith.

Apostles. Early disciples of Christ, sent by him into the world to spread the message of the Gospel. The most famous were the original twelve apostles.

Apostles' Creed. *See* Creed.

Apostolic Fathers. The earliest Christian writings, after the New Testament, written in Greek by men ("fathers") who were leaders of the church.

Ascension. An immediate rise from earth to heaven. The term is used especially for Jesus and his mother, Mary.

Ash Wednesday. The first day of Lent, held as a day of fasting and repentance in Christian churches. Many Christians receive a mark of ashes on the forehead as a reminder of their mortality.

Baptism. A Christian ritual of initiation that represents a public declaration of faith. The person being baptized is partially or fully immersed in water, or water is poured on his or her forehead as a sign of new life in Christ and the regeneration of faith. Most churches baptize infants, but many Protestant churches do not.

Baptist. A form of Protestant Christianity emphasizing the independence of local church and the individual believer. Baptists believe that baptism should be reserved for adults.

B.C. Used in dates to indicate years before the birth of Jesus; now often being replaced by "B.C.E." for "Before the Common Era."

Benediction. The final blessing at a religious service.

Bible. The sacred text of Christians. The Christian Bible contains the Old and New Testaments. It comes from a Greek word meaning "the books." The plural "books" reminds us that originally each of the elements of the Bible was an individual book and that the Bible we use is a collection of books.

Bishop. The priest (ordained minister) in charge of a large area or city, who acts as a pastor and teacher for other church leaders.

Black Theology. Theology that emerged in the United States in the 1960s, affirming black humanity and emphasizing the liberation of black people from white racism and cultural domination.

Blasphemy. Language that abuses the name of God, Christ, or other holy things.

Calvinist. Refers to the religious ideas of the Reformed churches that were profoundly influenced by John Calvin.

Canon, canonical. A rule or principle for sacred things (as in canon law), or sometimes a person who enforces such rules (the canon of a cathedral). Used of the Sacred Scriptures, the canon is the approved list of sacred books; such writings are "canonical," that is, according to the canon.

Cardinal Virtues. In Christian ethics, the four virtues essential for growth in good moral character: wisdom, self-control, courage, and honesty. The word "cardinal" comes from a Latin word that means "hinge."

Catholic. From a Greek word meaning "universal." When not capitalized, this term refers to the entire Christian church; when capitalized, it usually refers to the Roman (or Latin) Catholic tradition within Christianity.

Charismatic. From the New Testament word for "gifts" (of the Holy Spirit). The charismatic movement that began in the 1960s brought a Pentecostal emphasis on spiritual gifts and contemporary worship forms to larger and older Christian denominations. Today charismatic congregations and leaders are found in churches of all types, Catholic and Protestant.

Christ. The Greek word for the Messiah or "anointed one," the savior who was promised by God to Israel.

Christendom. A term used to designate the union of church and kingdom as an organic whole, which began with the Christian Roman Empire and continues in some explicitly Christian nations. The word is also used to designate the political and social impact of the Christian religion.

Christian. A person who follows Jesus Christ as Lord. As an adjective, it refers to ideas and groups associated with him.

Christmas. The day on which Christians celebrate the birth of Jesus. It is celebrated on December 25 in Western churches and on January 6 by Eastern (Orthodox) churches. It is also observed as a short season between Advent and Epiphany.

Christology. The study of Jesus Christ, or Christian teachings about Jesus.

Church. The people of God who follow Jesus Christ; or a building in which they meet for worship.

Church History. The history of the Christian movement from the earliest times to today. It includes the Patristic, Medieval, and Modern periods.

Church of England. *See* Anglican.

Clergy. Those people in the church who are ordained as leaders to perform pastoral and sacramental functions.

Confession. Also known in some churches as the sacrament of penance or reconciliation. This is the personal acknowledgment, made either in private or in public, of one's sin.

Confirmation. A practice whereby a mature Christian, baptized as an infant, publicly acknowledges acceptance of Christian faith and the vows of baptism.

Congregation. The corporate gathering of Christians in the worship service.

Congregationalist. Name given to the body of Protestant churches, deriving from seventeenth-century English separatists, that affirm the importance and autonomy of the local congregation.

Convent. A community of nuns, or the buildings in which they live.

Council of Chalcedon. One of the early ecumenical councils, held in 451 A.D. This council defined Jesus as one person with two natures, who is both fully human and fully divine. This became the standard Christian view.

Council of Trent. A theological council (1545–63) held by the Roman Catholic Church as a response to the challenges of the Protestant reformers and to further the Catholic Counter-Reformation.

Counter-Reformation. See Reformation.

Covenant. A special relationship or contract between God and his people.

Creed. A formal definition or summary of the Christian faith held in common by many or most Christians. The most important creeds are the Nicene Creed (dating back to A.D. 325) and the shorter Apostles' Creed (found in early forms dating back to about A.D. 390).

Deacons. Those who serve in helping offices or as other officers in the church, different from priest or pastor. The word "deacon" derives from a Greek word meaning "to serve."

Denominations. This term is used to designate the many different kinds of Christian tradition and church organizations. Some examples are Russian Orthodox, Methodist, Lutheran, and Roman Catholic.

Disciples. Followers of a teacher, especially followers of Jesus.

Doctrine. A statement of belief or theory regarding a certain theological issue. When making this statement, one pays attention to Scripture, tradition, and the prevailing beliefs of the day.

Dogma. An official or authoritative doctrine of the church, usually taught by a council of bishops as something necessary to be believed.

Easter. The most joyous season of the Christian calendar. On Easter Day the church celebrates Jesus' resurrection. The Easter season extends from Easter Sunday until the day of Pentecost.

Elders. A designation often used for important lay leaders in the local church organization.

Epiphany. A season in the Christian calendar when the church celebrates God coming into the world. The word "epiphany" means a personal revelation of the divine (in this case, the Christian God).

Episcopalian. *See* Anglican.

Essenes. Ultraconservative Jewish sect at the time of Jesus that withdrew to live in desert communities. The Essenes wrote the Dead Sea Scrolls.

Eucharist. *See* Holy Communion.

Evangelism. Telling others about the good news of Christ and inviting them to become disciples. The word comes from a Greek term for "good news," or Gospel.

Faith. Belief in, trust in, and a commitment to God. In the case of Christians, this faith is in God as revealed and known in Jesus Christ.

Feminist Theology. Theology that seeks to show how the understanding of God, Scripture, and Christianity, which predominantly has been interpreted and developed by and for men, must include the full humanity and experience of women.

Gentiles. Non-Jewish people.

Good Friday. The Friday before Easter. It is a special day for Christians as they remember the suffering and crucifixion of Jesus Christ.

Gospel. The message of good news about salvation in Jesus Christ.

Gospels. The first four books of the New Testament. These writings, called the Gospels of Matthew, Mark, Luke, and John, tell the story of Jesus.

Hebrew. The language or the people of ancient Israel.

Heresy. Teachings that are condemned by the church as false and harmful to faith.

Holy Communion. Also called the Eucharist or the Lord's Supper. This ritual of bread and wine is a major sacrament of the church, originally instituted by Jesus on the night before his crucifixion.

Holy Week. The week of festivals commemorating the last days of Jesus Christ on earth, ending with the celebration of his resurrection on Easter Sunday. This week includes Palm Sunday, Maundy (or Holy) Thursday, and Good Friday.

Huguenots. Name given to Calvinists in France in the sixteenth and seventeenth centuries.

Hymns. Songs that are sung as part of Christian worship. Traditionally, hymns are collected into books called "hymnals."

Icons. Images of Jesus Christ and of saints, which are often found in Christian churches, especially Orthodox ones.

Incarnate. The condition of being embodied in human nature and form. Christian theology holds that in the person of Jesus of Nazareth, God became incarnate.

Islam. The religious faith, traditions, and lifestyle of Muslims. Muslims worship God under the name Allah and follow the teachings of the prophet Muhammad. Their holy book is the Qur'an (often spelled "Koran" in older books).

Judaism. The faith of the Hebrew people. The Bible reports several sects existing within Judaism at the time of Jesus, including Pharisees, Sadducees, and Zealots.

Laity. Literally means "people," from the Greek word *laos*. This term is used for the people of the church who are not ordained as clergy.

Lay. See Laity.

Lent. From an Old English word meaning "spring." It is the season before Easter, the period when many Christians fast and pray as a way of remembering the suffering and fasting of Jesus for forty days in the wilderness.

Liberation Theology. A theological movement that developed in Latin America in the late 1960s, stressing the need to listen to the voice of the poor and the need for political action aimed at liberating the poor from poverty and oppression.

Liturgy. Refers to both the shape of the worship service and the elements within it, such as prayers and sacramental texts.

Lutheran. The name given to followers of Martin Luther, father of the Protestant Reformation.

Martyrs. From a Greek word meaning "witnesses." Martyrs are people who were tortured or killed for refusing to compromise or deny their faith.

Mass. An assembly of people worshiping together. This term usually is used especially in the Roman Catholic Church to designate the service of Word and Sacrament (Holy Communion) that is its most common form of worship.

Medieval. Having to do with the Middle Ages. This is a period of time in European history beginning roughly in the sixth century and ending with the Renaissance in the fifteenth century.

Mennonites. Name given to the largest group of Anabaptist churches in North America; the followers of Menno Simons (1496–1561), a Dutch Protestant reformer.

Messiah. A Hebrew word meaning "anointed one." It is the equivalent of the New Testament word "Christ."

Methodist. See Wesleyan.

Missions. The service and calling of the church to and for the world, in the name of Christ and out of love for God and the neighbor. Missionaries (people in mission) do acts of evangelism and other works of compassion.

Modern. The period of church history starting after the Reformation, generally considered to begin in 1517.

Monastery. A community of monks, or the buildings in which they live together.

Monotheists. People who believe that there is only one God. These people are different from henotheists, who worship one god without denying the existence of others.

Nicene Creed. *See* Creed.

Order, Religious. A spiritual, social, and economic community of women or men, usually with a special purpose or mission within a larger church body.

Orthodox. A term meaning "right belief." This word also is used as a name to refer to a group of ancient Eastern churches, such as the Greek Orthodox Church.

Pagan. A person who is not a worshiper of the God of Jews and Christians, and who thus worships other gods or none at all.

Palm Sunday. The Sunday that begins Holy Week. On Palm Sunday the triumphal entry of Jesus into Jerusalem is recalled, when his followers laid palm branches on his path.

Papacy. The office of the pope, or having to do with his office.

Patriarch. The founding fathers of Israel. The word comes from a Greek term meaning "father." The spiritual leaders of Eastern Orthodox churches are also called patriarchs.

Patristic. The period of the first five hundred years of church history.

Pentecost. Originally a Jewish agricultural festival of thanksgiving. In the Christian church Pentecost (also called "Whitsunday") occurs fifty days after Easter and is observed as the day when Jesus Christ sent the Holy Spirit to his followers. The season of Pentecost is the longest one of the church year, extending from May or June through the first Sunday of Advent.

Pentecostal. A twentieth-century movement within Protestant Christianity that emphasizes the power and work of the Holy Spirit. In the book of Acts, the Holy Spirit fell upon the first Christians on the day of Pentecost.

Pharisees. The group of first-century Jews closest to the religion of Jesus himself. This group was a conservative movement, concerned to protect the unique identity of Hebrew faith and Jewish laws in the face of the encroachments of Greek and Roman culture.

Pope. A title for the bishop of Rome, and the spiritual head of the Roman Catholic Church. He is considered by many to be the chief pastor of the church on earth, the "vicar of Christ."

Prayer. The act of talking to and listening for God. This is how Christians convey confession, requests, intercessions, thanksgiving, and other such communications to God.

Presbyterian. Name given to Protestant churches, first organized in Scotland, that traditionally are Calvinistic in doctrine.

Protestant. Word used to name families of Christian churches that are neither Eastern Orthodox nor Roman Catholic. These churches have a great variety of histories and traditions, but they all have their roots in the "protests" against the Roman Catholic Church in the sixteenth century. *See also* Reformation.

Psalms. Songs of praise, confession, and lament in the Old Testament. The Psalms have always been part of the prayer and worship of the church.

Puritans. Followers of an English form of Calvinism; powerful in the seventeenth century and influential in the development of Christianity in North America. Puritans believed in strict rules of conduct and simple forms of worship.

Quakers. See Society of Friends.

Rabbi. The teacher who leads a Jewish congregation.

Reformation. The period in sixteenth- and seventeenth-century Europe when Protestants sought to reform the church and Catholics engaged in a response. The Reformation's beginning usually is attributed to Martin Luther (1483–1546), and the Catholic reaction to the Reformation often is referred to as the Counter-Reformation.

Reformed. The church tradition that came about from the Protestant Reformation; also used for the chiefly Calvinist Protestant churches that formed in various European countries.

Religion. A distinctive way of life that involves special practices and rituals, along with associated beliefs about the world and God or Ultimate Reality. Not all religions believe in gods, but all religions have some kind of worldview, or philosophy of life.

Renaissance. The revival of classical culture in Europe following the Middle Ages; from a French word meaning "rebirth."

Resurrection. The act of being raised from the dead to immortal life. Jesus was the first to be resurrected; Christians believe that they too will be resurrected.

Ritual. Traditional practice or ceremony, included in almost every Christian worship service, that holds symbolic or spiritual meaning. Four of the most common Christian rituals are Bible reading, preaching, baptism, and Holy Communion.

Sabbath. The Jewish day of rest — the seventh day — as commanded in the Old Testament.

Sacraments. Sacred rituals of the Christian church. Sacraments use physical means to signify and convey supernatural grace. Christian churches differ over the number and meaning of sacraments and whether they were instituted by Jesus or are creations of the church to aid in worshiping God.

Sadducees. Members of a Jewish movement at the time of Jesus, chiefly located in cities. The Sadducees were favorable to collaboration with the Roman government and Greek culture, and often were members of the ruling class in Judea.

Salvation. Deliverance by God from the power of sin and death.

Sanctuary. The central part of a church or a temple, where the people gather to worship God.

Second Vatican Council. The major worldwide council of the Roman Catholic Church in the twentieth century, held in four October-to-December periods of the years 1962–65. Convened by Pope John XXIII, it resulted in the revision of most of the liturgy, the replacement of Latin with vernacular languages in rites, and the beginning of more open relationships with other Christian churches, with Jews, and with followers of other religious traditions.

Separatist. One who secedes or advocates separation, especially from an established church or other religious group.

Sermon. A religious speech in the service of worship, explaining the meaning for today of a passage from the Bible; also called a "homily."

Sin. Wrong attitudes or actions, contrary to God's will, that separate human beings from God.

Society of Friends. A radical separatist Christian movement, founded in seventeenth-century England by George Fox, that emphasizes the "inner light" of Christ in every person; more commonly known as the Quakers.

Symbol. One thing that represents and points to another thing.

Theology. The study of God; from Greek words meaning, literally, "talk about God."

Traditions. Wisdom and teachings developed in a religion and handed down from generation to generation.

Trinity. Refers to the "one" God of the Christians, who is a unity of "three persons": Father, Son, and Holy Spirit.

Vices. Bad habits that lead us to evil deeds. Vices stand in opposition to virtues.

Virtues. Habits of the soul, or character traits, that lead us to good deeds. Traditionally, seven virtues have been a central focus of Christian ethics.

Wesleyan. Protestant tradition stemming from the revival under the English evangelist John Wesley in the eighteenth century; also called Methodist.

Zealots. Members of a radical Jewish movement around the time of Jesus that fought against Roman rule in Palestine.

Index

*Note: Entries marked with an asterisk (*)
are also listed in the Glossary.*

155